Value and Validity in Action Research

A Guidebook for Reflective Practitioners

Eileen M. Schwalbach

A SCARECROWEDUCATION BOOK

The Scarecrow Press, Inc.
Lanham, Maryland, and Oxford
2003

A SCARECROWEDUCATION BOOK

Published in the United States of America
by Scarecrow Press, Inc.
An imprint of The Rowman & Littlefield Publishing Group, Inc.
4501 Forbes Boulevard, Suite 200, Lanham, MD 20706
www.scarecroweducation.com

PO Box 317
Oxford
OX2 9RU, UK

British Library Cataloguing in Publication Information Available

Library of Congress Cataloging-in-Publication Data

Schwalbach, Eileen M.
  Value and validity in action research : a guidebook for reflective
practitioners / Eileen M. Schwalbach.
      p. cm.
"A ScarecrowEducation book."
Includes bibliographical references.
  ISBN 1-57886-017-2 (pbk. : alk. paper)
  1. Action research in education—United States. 2. Effective
teaching—United States. I. Title.
  LB1028.24 .S47 2003
  370'.7'2—dc21

                                                              2003003858

∞™ The paper used in this publication meets the minimum requirements of
American National Standard for Information Sciences—Permanence of
Paper for Printed Library Materials, ANSI/NISO Z39.48-1992.
Manufactured in the United States of America.

Contents

Foreword

The term "action research" combines two concepts that too often are disconnected. "Research," for example, is popularly seen as the province of persons in lab coats, carefully managing variables in laboratory situations. And while educational researchers may not always fit that stereotype, we do receive the perennial criticism that educational research is not applied because it is not seen as relevant in the "real" classroom.

Adding "action" to research connotes a different sense of inquiry, one that is carried out in the classroom setting and recognizes both the context and the complexity of the teacher's practice. This kind of research puts the teacher in the researcher role. The relevance of this kind of research to the teacher's work is obvious; the benefits are just beginning to be understood in classrooms around the country.

Three key benefits of teachers engaging in action research stand out. First, action research supports student learning. A teacher who raises questions about student learning and systematically seeks answers in the classroom can more effectively meet the needs of students. The teacher goes farther than before in exploring possible ways to reach students.

Second, action research sparks teacher learning. A teacher who raises questions and seeks answers through reading, conversations with other teachers, courses, and systematic study in classrooms is growing as a professional and expanding his or her professional scope. Action research can be seen as an antidote to teachers who use the same lesson plans for thirty years.

Third, action research contributes to the profession. Teachers who raise questions and carry out action research contribute to professional discourse, whether through sharing informally with others or through formal publication of work. Their questions resonate with those of others, who then explore the implications of the researchers' work in their own classrooms.

This book provides a clear and helpful way for teachers to become engaged in action research. Eileen Schwalbach skillfully guides the reader through the processes involved in raising questions, exploring the literature, developing a research design, and interpreting results. Her approach makes this book useful for practicing teachers. In each section, she raises questions or provides examples that help the reader to clearly visualize the process. In fact, the reader can use this book as a workbook—in the best sense of that term—a book that readers can work their way through so that at the end they have the skills that have been discussed, rather than just knowing about them.

Finally, this book provides, in teachers' own voices, a sense of the power of action research. Teachers share their experiences in each part of the process, providing a concrete sense of not only the process but also the impact action research has on their lives as teaching professionals. Every teacher can find an echo in these teachers' words, which serve as reminders of why teachers chose the profession and its call to ongoing growth.

Mary E. Diez, Ph.D.
Graduate Dean, Alverno College

Acknowledgments

I have been inspired to write this book by those whom I have taught and those who have taught me; in many cases these are the same people. I have learned as much from my students as they have learned from me. The four teachers whose words resonate throughout the book represent the many students whom I have had the privilege to teach. My colleagues at Mount Mary College, as well as Dr. Beverly Cross at the University of Wisconsin, Milwaukee, and Dr. Mary Diez at Alverno College, have supported my work. My family and friends have provided unfailing encouragement.

1

Introduction to Action Research

- Have you ever tried something new in your classroom and wondered if it really promoted student learning?
- Is there something that you'd like to change about your instructional strategies to better help students learn?
- Do you want to make any changes in the curriculum to facilitate learning?
- Have you ever been frustrated by changing fads in education? Maybe you've tried something, only to discover that it's out of favor the next year.

If you've answered "yes" to any of these questions, action research will help you try ideas in your classroom, find out if they work, and know that these ideas aren't merely passing fads, but rather effective ways of helping children to learn.

Action research is the process of investigating something you are doing in your own classroom. Grady (1998) puts it this way: "Action research is reflective inquiry undertaken by educators in order to better understand the education environment and to improve practice" (p. 43).

There are several important aspects of these definitions. First, you're the researcher as well as the teacher. You're looking at what's happening in your classroom and your school. Sometimes there is a large gap between what university researchers are studying and your practice. Some teachers feel alienated from scholarly research because there is a separation between theory and practice. In fact, the kind of knowledge that is most helpful to teachers, "called 'craft knowledge' . . . is characterized more by its concreteness and contextual richness than its generalizability and context independence" (Hiebert, Gallimore, and Stigler, 2002, p. 3), the characteristics of scholarly research. In action research *you're* deciding what needs to be studied. Maybe you want to know if using a writers' workshop will improve *your* students' essays, or perhaps you're interested in increasing *your* students' depth of understanding in math by integrating math and science. Action research unites theory and practice, as you become the researcher in your classroom.

Second, action research involves investigating something. Through a systematic process of inquiry, data are collected. These data are then analyzed. You draw conclusions about what worked, what didn't, what you should do next. Good teachers try new methods and curriculums all the time and have a sense of whether or not they are helping students to learn. Now you'll collect data in a systematic way and have evidence as to whether or not your ideas really do achieve the outcomes that you want.

Third, the result of action research is improved practice. You'll be a better teacher because you will have gained insights into student learning, or maybe you'll find that you should stop doing something because it isn't effective. In either case you'll be a more reflective teacher. You'll see problems as opportunities to try something different and investigate whether or not it's effective. Your students will also benefit from your action research as their understanding deepens and their classroom is enriched by your efforts.

The value of action research, therefore, is in helping teachers become better teachers, so that students will have more meaningful and engaging learning opportunities. Although action research can be used to investigate questions that don't deal directly with student learning (e.g., How can a teacher create a useful professional development plan?), this book will address projects that directly focus on student learning.

Some critics have questioned the ability of teachers to do this kind of research and get valid results (Hodgkinson, 1982; Huberman, 1996). They believe teachers lack the research skills needed to do valid research. The purpose of this book is to help teachers gain the knowledge and skills necessary to design valuable action research projects that will produce valid findings.

HISTORY OF ACTION RESEARCH

The beginnings of action research can be traced to several sources. The term "action research" was first used by Kurt Lewin, a social psychologist, in 1944 to describe a cyclical process of planning, implementing, monitoring, and evaluating (Kemmis, 1982). Lewin used this methodology to address social problems caused by industrialization, such as hunger and unsafe working conditions. Although Lewin coined the term, others had promoted the use of action research before Lewin. John Collier, commissioner of Indian affairs for the U.S. Bureau of Indian Affairs from 1933 to 1945, is credited with formulating the idea of action research as a means of responding to the social problems of American Indians (Kemmis, 1982). Other early theoretical influences include John Dewey's advocacy of teachers mining their own practice (Dewey, 1929).

Although action research did not spring from educators,

> The idea of action research was absorbed into education almost as soon as it originated. Lewin himself worked in action research programs with teachers and teacher educators. But his ideas were taken up most evidently in the work of the Horace Mann-Lincoln Institute of Teachers' [*sic*] College, Columbia University. The Institute was already engaged in curriculum development for social reconstruction and collaborative research with teachers, schools and school districts. Action research was a method which synthesised [*sic*] a range of contemporary concerns and provided a dynamic for collaborative programs of action in schools. (Kemmis, 1982, p. 17)

Stephen Corey, the dean of Teachers College, is credited with using action research "to improve the rate of curriculum change in schools and to reduce the gap between research knowledge and instructional practice in classrooms" (Zeichner and Noffke, 2001, p. 301).

By the 1950s action research was in decline. There were many reasons for this, one of which was an attack on the methods used by action researchers. Hodgkinson (1982) criticized teachers' lack of training in research, which he believed rendered them incapable of conducting rigorous scientific inquiry. According to Sanford (1981) its decline was a result of an increasing separation of theoretical research and practice. In the post-Sputnik era, academic researchers were heavily funded to do large, scientific studies, and the small, reflective action research projects faded from view.

The 1960s saw a resurgence in action research in Great Britain. By the 1980s action research had reemerged in the United States. Multiple influences affected this new movement. Among them were the growing recognition of qualitative research as an accepted methodology and the inclusion of action research in teacher education programs (Zeichner and Noffke, 2001). Today action research has support around the world.

ACTION RESEARCH VS. RESEARCH IN TEACHING

To better understand action research, it's useful to distinguish it from another kind of research. Research about teachers and classroom practice done by others (i.e., university or foundation researchers) is called research in teaching. Cochran-Smith and Lytle (1993) clarify important differences between action research and research in teaching. Action research is intended to improve practice in a local context, whereas research in teaching generates theory that eventually may filter down to improve practice. Action research questions spring from concerns of teachers, while research in teaching questions emerge from theory within a discipline. The results of action research pertain to the specific context of a teacher's classroom, while the results of research in teaching are intended for larger audiences.

Although there are similarities between action research, done by teachers in their schools, and research in teaching, done by researchers in other people's classrooms, there are important differences.

Let's look at an example.

As an action researcher you may notice a lack of cooperation in your classroom. You decide to teach social skills by using cooperative learning. You read the literature to see what others have found about cooperation. You decide what behaviors you are looking for. You create lessons in which you teach, monitor, and process these skills. During the time period of the study, you teach the lessons as well as collect data to see if the lessons are effective. You keep a journal in which you note cooperative behaviors. Maybe you use a tally sheet to note the frequency of these behaviors. Perhaps you interview your students to see if they are noticing more cooperation in the classroom. If you found that these lessons worked, you would use them again with other classes. Perhaps you'd share them with your fellow teachers.

A professionally trained researcher would approach the problem differently. She would be familiar with the literature on cooperative learning. There might be a gap in the research—topics that haven't been investigated. Or there might be studies that need to be replicated. Her concern would be extending the body of research. She might decide to do a quantitative study and use a control and an experimental group. She would carefully control the variables because she would want her findings to be generalizable to other classrooms.

QUALITATIVE VS. QUANTITATIVE RESEARCH

Action research, as well as research in teaching, uses both qualitative and quantitative designs. A contentious debate has been waged in the academy over the merits of these two types of research. While they spring from different philosophical positions and serve different purposes, both can be useful in action research (Glickman, Gordon, and Ross-Gordon, 1998).

Philosophical Assumptions

Quantitative research is based on the belief that knowledge is fixed. Because it's not relative or culturally bound, you can discover it, measure it, and use it to predict future behavior. The researcher must be objective in gathering and analyzing data so that the results will be valid. If a well-designed quantitative study shows that a certain strategy improves student achievement in reading, you would expect that strategy to work with other children.

Qualitative research, on the other hand, is based on the assumption that knowledge is relative; it is changing, depending on the people and the setting involved. Qualitative researchers believe that it's impossible to be totally objective. They think that a certain degree of subjectivity exists in all research. Knowledge is seen as complex, and this complexity cannot be broken into discrete variables that can be studied or controlled. (Think of all the variables that affect your students' learning—time of day, time of year, home life, etc.) Qualitative researchers study research questions holistically. For example, a qualitative study might look at a few children and describe how each one is learning to read when using a certain reading strategy. This in-depth study would be conducted over time and would be reported in a rich narrative.

Purpose

Because of their differing assumptions, these two kinds of research have different purposes. Quantitative research seeks to quantify and measure data. The end purpose, then, is to use these data to generalize to a larger population and make predictions about future behaviors. Some quantitative studies are designed to show a cause-effect relationship between two variables. Policy makers value these kinds of studies for just these reasons. If a certain project is to be funded, they want reassurance that the project will yield the expected results.

Qualitative researchers describe what they have found in great detail. This rich description tries to capture the truthfulness and complexity of the situation. While these studies are insightful and helpful in thinking about other contexts, they are not intended to show causality or to predict behaviors in other settings. However, they can provide useful insights for practicing teachers.

Different Kinds of Questions

As you might expect, these two kinds of research pose different kinds of research questions.

Quantitative researchers ask questions that can be answered with quantitative data. If you want to know whether using math manipulatives increases student achievement in math, you have to be able to measure achievement, probably by giving an objective test. But what if you want to know if using these manipulatives has deepened students' understanding of certain math concepts? It may be better to do a qualitative study in which you describe students' responses to math problems.

Qualitative researchers begin their research with an open-ended question. As they do their research, they may learn things that lead them to change their questions. As qualitative researchers collect data and begin to notice patterns, other questions may emerge.

Quantitative Questions	*Qualitative Questions*
• answered with data that measure	• answered with data that describe

- are more narrowly focused
- don't change during the study

- are open-ended
- may change as you collect data

Exercise A. Would these questions be better answered with quantitative or qualitative methods? Give an explanation for each answer. (Possible answers are given at the end of the questions.)

1. How can performance-based assessment be used to reflect students' understanding of scientific concepts?
2. How will having students write for authentic audiences affect their motivation?
3. Will the use of graphic organizers improve student achievement on unit tests in history?
4. How can a teacher use students' interests and experiences to motivate them to learn?
5. Will learning keyboarding improve students' spatial reasoning?
6. Write two research questions, one quantitative and one qualitative.

Possible answers for exercise A. Additional explanations may be correct.

1. Qualitative   The question asks *how* performance-based assessment can be used to ascertain student understanding. You would have to define "understanding" and describe the depth and breadth of the understanding. If you wanted to know only *whether* understanding was affected, you might use a rubric to quantify the understanding. However, you still would want to describe what and how the students were learning through this kind of assessment.
2. Qualitative   It would be very difficult to quantify motivation. You might interview students about their motivation, observe their nonverbal behaviors, and look at the quality of the work. These factors could be described in the findings.
3. Quantitative   Because you have a test score for each unit, you could measure improvement or lack of it. You would have to be careful that the tests and the material in the units weren't getting easier or more difficult.
4. Qualitative   Because the question is a *how* question, you will need to describe the different ways in which students' interests and experiences have motivated them.

5. Quantitative   If you find a way to measure spatial reasoning, you can determine whether there is a relationship between it and keyboarding skills.

ACTION RESEARCH

You can see that, as an action researcher, you will do work that is more closely allied to qualitative research. As the teacher-researcher you will never achieve the objectivity that quantitative researchers demand. And you don't want to generalize your results to other students. You just want to know what kind of impact your teaching has had on student learning. As you share your results with other teachers, you may encourage them to try what has worked for you; however, you aren't promising the same results.

You can use some quantitative methods, however. For example, you may do a survey as part of your study. Perhaps you'll look at the scores on objective tests. These methods will be discussed further in chapter 4.

Validity in Action Research

Action research is an important tool in individual professional development as well as in whole school reform. It is widely used in graduate programs as a capstone project, as well as by schools and school districts to encourage reform. Individual teachers, as well as groups of teachers, are undertaking action research to increase student learning. As more teachers use this methodology, serious questions need to be raised: How can teachers ensure that their results are trustworthy? Are teachers drawing conclusions supported by their data? These questions address the issue of validity.

The debate about validity is complex and contentious. Because of the different perspectives of university researchers, validity in action research has many different definitions. (See Zeichner and Noffke [2001] for a thorough explanation.) For the purposes of this book "validity" refers to the accuracy of the claims that you make regarding your findings.

Action researchers can address validity issues using techniques similar to those of qualitative researchers. However, the possibility of validity in qualitative research has been a controversial issue. Guba (1981) speaks to the concerns of quantitative researchers who question the ability of qualitative researchers to establish validity. Guba argues that qualitative researchers need to ensure credibility by considering all the complexities that exist in the study, to understand that the results are specific to the context of the study, to establish the stability of the data by triangulation, and to collect objective data. Maxwell (1992) examines the need for factual, nonevaluative accuracy in the account of the study, for recognition of the participants' perspectives, for the ability of the study to adequately explain the phenomenon being examined, and for limitations on the degree to which the study can be generalized. Goetz and LeCompte (1984) state that to ensure validity "the design [of the study] should fit lines of inquiry" (p. 245). In other words, the study must be thoughtfully designed and implemented in order to get accurate findings.

Action researchers can apply many of these principles to their studies. Teacher-researchers must understand that their results cannot be generalized to other contexts. They must recognize their own subjectivity yet take precautions to be as objective as possible. They must ask questions that can be answered by collecting data that are gathered using well-designed procedures and by analyzing those data carefully and thoroughly.

A key way to ensure validity is by triangulation of data (Mills, 2000). Teacher-researchers need at least three ways in which to collect data in order to determine the accuracy of their conclusions. Like all qualitative researchers, teachers need to keep a journal in which they write objective and reflective comments. They can collect student work, videotape and audiotape class discussions and work, create checklists, conduct interviews, take surveys, and give pre- and posttests. Finally, the results are recorded, using thick, rich description. In that way other teachers who read the findings will be able to ascertain whether or not the project is applicable to them and their students.

These and other ways to ensure validity will be discussed in the following chapters. As an addition to the explanations that the chapters will provide, you will meet four teachers who grappled with issues regarding value and validity as they designed and implemented their action research projects. In each of the chapters these teachers will share the experiences they had as they worked through this rigorous and rewarding process. Each of them represents a different grade level and subject. Their projects may be similar to or different from yours; however, they all have valuable lessons to teach us.

TEACHER VOICES

Deb: Integrating Calculus and Physics

Deb is a mathematics teacher at a religious high school in a large metropolitan city in the Midwest. This school is the only school where Deb has taught. She has worked there for fifteen years. This school mainly serves middle-class students; however, approximately 10 percent of the student body is made up of low-income students who attend through the state-sponsored school choice program. In Deb's study she worked with thirty-two seniors in advanced placement calculus, twenty-two males and ten females.

She provided this high-achieving class with concrete examples from their physics class to give them a contextually rich environment in which to explore the abstractions of calculus. Students discovered connections between the physics concepts of position, velocity, and acceleration and the calculus concepts of function, derivative, and antiderivative. The qualitative study sought to describe several critical aspects of understanding: students' ability to explain concepts and procedures, to apply concepts in a physics context, and to explore their own learning.

Jen: Metacognition and Narrative Writing

Jen has been an English teacher for the past nine years at the high school where Deb teaches. In her action research project, she taught ninth graders metacognitive strategies for planning, writing, and revising narrative essays. Her class consisted of eight males and twelve females. Their reading scores ranged from the third to the seventy-fifth percentile on the placement test for incoming freshmen. Five of the students received tuition assistance from the state through the school choice program.

Jen's students learned effective planning strategies for their narrative writing, including setting specific goals and identifying strengths and weaknesses. Using Sandra Cisneros's *House on Mango Street* as a model, the students planned, wrote, and revised a series of vignettes.

Sharon: Intergenerational Friendly Visit Program

Sharon, a Title I support teacher at a suburban K-5 school in the Midwest, has been a teacher for thirteen years. Her school is a neighborhood school that attracts 15 percent of its students from outside the district. The majority of the students are middle class, but 18 percent are low income.

Sharon's study described the effects of an intergenerational friendly visit program on the attitudes toward elders of one fourth-grade class. This class consisted of twenty-two students, eleven boys and eleven girls. Two of the students had been identified as learning disabled, one as gifted, and two as English language learners.

Students visited with their elder "special friends" at a nursing home every week for five months. In-class lessons regarding students' knowledge and attitudes toward elders prepared students for the visits. The students and the elders worked on projects that addressed curricular objectives in guidance, health, and communicative arts. Together they played games, shared reading, and decorated pumpkins, clay pots, and cookies. For each of the elders the students created a "living history book" that chronicled his or her life.

Lenore: Literacy through Play

Lenore, a teacher for seven years, works with kindergartners in a public elementary school in a suburb that adjoins a large metropolitan area in the Midwest. Her neighborhood school is primarily middle class. She implemented her study in a morning and in an afternoon four-year-old kindergarten. The morning group had twenty students, ten boys and ten girls. Two students participated in the English as a second language program. In the afternoon class, there were twenty-four students, ten boys and fourteen girls. Two of the students had been identified as having special needs.

Lenore wanted to know whether providing her students with literacy-enriched play centers and modeling literacy behaviors would increase their engagement in literacy behaviors. She set up four centers, the block area, the writing center, the living center, and the thematic center, that changed focus every three or four weeks. Each center was stocked with literacy props like paper, pencils, books, and signs.

CONCLUSION

As you explore the action research process, you will be following these four teachers as they proceed on their journey of discovery. They will learn about their students and about themselves as teachers. Their lives will be transformed as they become researchers in their own classrooms.

2

Finding a Problem

"**P**roblem" is a research term. It refers to the subject under investigation. What do you want to look at? Another definition of "problem" is something for which you don't know the answer. There are many reasons to do action research. When you're choosing a problem to investigate, you might want to consider the following:

- What do you feel passionate about?
- What will make you a better teacher?
- What needs of your students are not being met?
- Why are some of your students achieving and others not?
- What do you want your students to know, understand, and do better than they currently do?
- What can you investigate in the amount of time you have?

Choose a topic that will make a difference in your life and the lives of the children you teach. How valuable will your project be in providing a better education for your students? Think about what things have the greatest impact on student learning in your classroom. As you provide this input, you will be looking systematically at the student learning that is occurring. As you reflect on this student learning, you will see how you can continue to improve your practice and provide even better instruction. This cyclical process of reflection and action is at the heart of effective teaching.

Here are some topics you might consider:

- curriculum revision
- instructional strategies
- assessment
- problem-solving skills
- communication skills
- integrating the curriculum
- parent relationships
- community involvement
- special education needs
- diversity issues

Exercise A. Answer the following questions.

1. What other topics would be appropriate for action research?
2. What kind of input could you provide for your students that would improve student learning and in turn make you a better teacher? This could be your topic.

NARROWING THE PROBLEM

Once you have a topic, you have a general idea of what you want to study. However, you need to narrow your focus. If you're planning a trip to Colorado, you need to decide what part of the state you want to visit, and eventually what activities you want to do. It's the same for an action research project. If you don't have a specific focus, your project can meander aimlessly, and you can waste valuable time.

When you're narrowing your topic, be careful that you are choosing a focus that will help your students to learn. Hiebert, Gallimore, and Stigler (2002) cite the example of faculty at an elementary school who wanted to improve the reading readiness skills of low-income, Spanish-speaking kindergarten students. They decided to teach phonics, using a variety of methods. When the children didn't learn phonics, the teachers used different strategies to teach the same content. What they didn't realize was that phonics was not the key to reading for these children. By doing some professional reading, you will be able to assess how effective your methods will be. Your action research project will be informed by scholarly research. (Reviewing the scholarly literature will be discussed in the next chapter.)

Exercise B. Think about the following questions to help you narrow your problem.

1. Consider a topic—for instance, integrating the curriculum. What is your topic? (See figure 2.1 to narrow your topic.)
2. What do you want to know about your topic? For example, do you want to know whether using problem-based learning deepens student understanding in science?
3. What are you going to do to answer your question(s)? In other words, what's the "action" in your action research? For example, are you going to teach a unit in which students investigate real-life problems?
4. How long will this "action" take you? Is this time frame realistic?
5. How will you assess your students' and your own learning? For example, will you examine student work to assess student understanding?

What is your topic?	
What do you want to know about your topic?	
What are you going to do to answer this question?	
How long will this project take?	
How will you assess learning?	

Figure 2.1.   Narrow Your Topic

By answering the questions in figure 2.1, you have begun to conceptualize your action research project. Your ideas may change as you work through the process; however, these exercises provide a start. The following chapters will take you deeper into the process.

NEED FOR THE PROJECT

Action research projects should make an important contribution to student learning as well as teacher learning. Consider the need for this project by answering these questions.

- Why is it important to do this project?
- What conditions or situations make this project significant?

Perhaps you notice an achievement gap between white students and students of color. Maybe your district has adopted a new textbook that will necessitate some changes in the curriculum. Maybe you'd like to increase your students' understanding by showing them connections between subjects.

Think about the needs that you have read about in research. For example, we know that girls' achievement in math and science drops off in high school. Maybe you want to investigate whether or not girls learn biology differently than boys. What are the needs in your district, your school, your classroom? Perhaps your school district is trying to raise its math scores on standardized tests, so this outcome has become a priority for your district. There is an obvious need for you as a classroom teacher to address this concern.

To investigate the need for your project at the national level, you can look at the results of the National Assessment of Educational Progress. Students across the country are tested in different subjects periodically. The results of "The Nation's Report Card" can be obtained on the Internet at NAEP:nces.ed.gov/nationsreportcard.

Exercise C. Freewrite and explain why this project is needed. By thinking about the need for the project, you are addressing concerns about the value of your project.

ASSUMPTIONS: YOUR PHILOSOPHY OF EDUCATION

Before you begin your study, you should consider the assumptions that underlie your project. These assumptions are beliefs that you will not need to verify with research. For example, do you believe that the role of the teacher is to dispense knowledge or to facilitate learning? The position that you take will serve as a lens through which you see your project. You need to be aware of your assumptions about teaching and learning and how they will influence your decisions about instruction, curriculum, assessment, motivation, and so forth.

Exercise D. What are your assumptions about the following?

- What kind of persons do you want your students to become?
- What should be taught in schools?
- What is the role of the teacher?
- What kind of classroom atmosphere best facilitates learning?
- What kinds of instructional strategies work best?
- Are there any other assumptions that you are making that are specific to your project?

When you have answered these questions, you should have a more explicit notion about the beliefs that underpin your teaching and that will undergird your action research project.

PARAMETERS

Now you need to think more specifically about your project. Think about the constraints of your project. You will have to do it within a certain time frame. You will have access to certain materials, but not others.

Exercise E. Answer the following questions about the parameters of your project.

1. Where will you do the project?
2. With which students will you do the project?
3. What is your time frame?

4. What instructional materials are available?

5. What other limitations will your project have?

TERMINOLOGY

All disciplines have their own terminology. In education we use terms like "intelligence," "creativity," and "learning styles." But what do we mean? Does "learning styles" refer to whether students learn better by seeing something rather than hearing it, or whether they are global or sequential learners, or whether they like a quiet or a noisy environment when they study? "Learning styles" could refer to all of these. Therefore, it's important to clarify exactly what you mean by a term.

Keep a list of terms that have multiple meanings or terms that may not be recognized by most educators. List a source for each of these terms. If you are using the term "intelligence," did you get your definition from Thorndike or Gardner or some other theorist? Your definition of "intelligence" makes a big difference in how you frame your study.

RESEARCH QUESTIONS

You have some preliminary questions. (See "Narrowing the Problem.") However, you may want to revise these questions. In fact, you can keep revising these questions throughout the project. As you collect data, you will get a better sense of what you really want to know. Sometimes qualitative researchers don't start with questions, but rather let them emerge from the data. These kinds of studies require long periods of research—something teachers don't have. That's why it's a good idea to choose more specific questions that will help you to focus your study. The following section will discuss criteria for writing good research questions.

Exercise F. Check your questions against the following criteria. Answer the following questions.

- *Is the question open-ended?* Don't ask questions that can be answered by a "yes" or "no" response. Sometimes you just need to change the wording. Which question is better?

Will cooperative learning affect students' ability to engage in academic discourse in social studies?

How will cooperative learning affect students' ability to engage in academic discourse in social studies?

The second question allows for a richer response. It requires the teacher-researcher to think about the quality as well as the quantity of students' verbal interactions.

• *Does the question assume an answer?* Which is better?

How will the use of a writers workshop improve students' writing?

How will the use of a writers workshop affect students' writing?

The first question assumes that the writers workshop approach will positively affect students' writing. The second does not. Remember that the merit of your project does not depend on finding something that yields positive results. Finding that something doesn't work is just as significant. Think about the research on prescription drugs. It's just as important to know what won't cure an illness as it is to know what will.

• *Does the question have appropriate scope—not too broad or too specific?* Which is best?

How will using guided reading affect students' scores on reading tests?

How will using guided reading help a teacher to meet the needs of individual students?

What will improve students' reading?

The second question allows the teacher-researcher to look at students' reading in a broader way than in the first question. She can use various assessments to determine whether or not students are learning to read. The third question is too broad. It does not suggest any methods for improving reading.

• *Is the question based in research literature?*

Immerse yourself in research literature before you refine your questions. What have professional researchers discovered about your topic? You may be interested in dividing your students into ability groups. What does the research literature have to say about this? Remember the case of the elementary teachers who persistently taught phonics to the Spanish-speaking kindergartners. Check that your methodology is sound.

- *Is the question stated clearly and concisely?* Which question is better?

What effect will connecting students' new learning to previous learning have on their new learning when a teacher uses brain-based strategies?

How can a teacher create lessons in language arts that will help students access background knowledge?

Although brain-based research supports tying new learning to old by accessing background knowledge, it is not necessary to add it to the question. Make your questions clear and concise. Avoid jargon.

- *Can the question be answered by collecting data?* Which question is better?

What is Howard Gardner's multiple intelligences theory?

How can a science teacher use multiple intelligences theory to meet the learning needs of diverse students?

The first question can be answered by reading books and articles about multiple intelligences theory. For the second question, you would have to use various kinds of assignments and assessments to discover the answer.

- *Is the question ethical?*

Make sure that you are not asking about something that could harm a child. For example, what could be the impact of labeling children as "low achieving"? Would it be ethical to use a method to teach reading that isn't supported by any research on teaching?

- *Is the connection between your "action" and your expected outcome strong enough?* Which question is better?

How will a parent education program affect students' reading achievement?

How can a teacher design a parent education program to help parents assist their children in reading?

Think about all the variables that affect children's reading achievement. Certainly an important one is what you do as a classroom teacher. How will you be able to tell what is causing the children's achievement to increase or decrease? Is it your lessons, or is it the input of the parents? The first question will not yield valid results because you'll never be able to tease apart the reasons for any improvement in reading. However, setting up a parent education program is a worthy goal. By changing the focus of the question, you'll be able come to some trustworthy conclusions.

- *Is the question significant?*

  This criterion addresses value. Are you asking a question that will yield information that will help you become a better teacher and your students become better learners? This book will help you to focus on student learning as you do your action research.

- *Is the question feasible?*

  The last criterion prompts you to look at your ability to accomplish your project in a reasonable amount of time. Schools are placing an increasing emphasis on standardized tests. Consider whether or not you can spend six to eight weeks on a specific unit. Some topics need this kind of development; however, you may not have the time to give every unit the depth of coverage you would like. For example, while the Holocaust is an important topic for study, you may not be able to ask a question about deep understanding in a unit that lasts only a few days. You may want to know how students understand metaphors, yet you may only have a day or two to work with this concept.

Exercise G. Check to see if your question meets these criteria. If not, revise your question.

My research question

- ___ is open-ended (not "yes"/"no")
- ___ is unbiased
- ___ has appropriate scope
- ___ reflects current research
- ___ is clear and specific
- ___ can be answered by collecting data
- ___ is ethical
- ___ has a strong connection between the "action" and the expected outcome
- ___ is significant
- ___ is feasible

TEACHER VOICES

By completing the exercises in this chapter, you have worked through the process of selecting a topic and thinking about how to turn this topic into an action research project. You will now hear the stories of the four teachers introduced in chapter 1. These stories in the teachers' own words are included at the end of each chapter to provide examples of how real teachers have undertaken the action research process. In these excerpts the teachers explain how they decided on the topics for their research projects. These are examples of projects with value and validity. Their value springs from the effects that the projects had on student learning. (Their validity will be discussed throughout the book.) These projects reflect a deep concern for addressing student needs by providing meaningful, authentic activities. By reading these stories, you will learn valuable lessons about choosing a topic and narrowing and focusing it to create a research question.

Deb: Looking for Solutions

At the point I began thinking about my research topic, I had been teaching calculus for about ten years. I had become increasingly aware of the fact that many students were in the habit of manipulating equations by rote rather than really understanding the mathematical concepts underlying the manipulations. I also realized that part of what made this possible was the fact that most of the problems presented in textbooks at that time were decontextualized. They were purely mathematical. Students were simply given an equation or expression which they would then manipulate mathematically to arrive at a solution. There weren't many "word problems" where students had to use information in the problem scenario to set up an expression, then manipulate it to find a solution which had a particular meaning in the context of the problem

Experiences of four students in my calculus class provided clear evidence of a pressing need to revitalize instruction in that area. The fact that these were students in calculus indicated that they had pursued a rigorous course of study in the area of mathematics. They had attained a degree of success in the subject as defined by their grades in previous mathematics courses, and all also were enrolled in honors physics.

Early in the school year, the first student, Jessica, and I were working through a problem involving a rational equation and absolute value. We had reached a point where she had to evaluate an equation when the variable took on certain values. At that point she asked, "Isn't there some way I can do this without thinking about it?" Jessica was, no doubt, not the only student in the class who preferred simply to manipulate a formula without ever attaching meaning to the process. This approach obviously had worked well for her in the past. After all, she had successfully reached the level of calculus. Jessica's question posed the first reason to rethink how mathematics is taught. Students need to really understand the concepts of mathematics in order to apply them. Without the understanding of key concepts, mathematics is merely a set of magical manipulations which produces a correct but meaningless result.

Robert presented the second need for a revision in calculus instruction. At the end of the first semester, students in calculus registered to take the advanced placement test that would be given later in the instructional process at the end of the school year. Robert insisted on registering for the test even though he had not been particularly successful in the course to that point. He explained that if he earned a satisfactory score on the test, he would never have to take a math course again in his life—at least not at the college he intended to attend. That benefit, he had determined, was definitely worth the money and the risk. Calculus, however, is not meant to be a terminal course in mathematics. Rather, it serves as the beginning of a sequence of professional courses that prepare students to assume competent roles in the technological and informational age. Most importantly, students need to recognize the value of mathematics and how it impacts other areas.

In contrast to Robert, the third student, Christopher, consistently earned high grades in math courses throughout his high school career. Christopher's achievement indicated that he was a logical candidate to perform well on the advanced placement test. Christopher's classmates prepared for the exam by forming study groups and working together on sample problems. They would often seek my help and advice. However, Christopher chose to study for the exam independently. Unfortunately, while the majority of his classmates achieved a score that earned them college credit, Christopher did not. Christopher's situation highlights the need for communication to be part of the learning process. In this situation, students who worked together with other students and with their teacher performed better than an accomplished student who chose to work alone.

On a much more positive note, the fourth need for new approaches to mathematics education was offered by Kathryn. Kathryn's physics teacher shared this anecdote with me. Groups of physics students were working collaboratively on a problem. The boys in Kathryn's group were working at the chalkboard, while the girls were organizing data at their desks. Part way through the problem, Kathryn noticed the gender-role distinction and stopped the group for a moment to point out what had happened and make reference to an article she had chosen to read for calculus class which discussed the differences in learning styles of males and females. Explicit connections between classes and subjects enhance the learning process and often make it more enjoyable for the students. Some students, like Kathryn, grasp the connections on their own. But many students need to develop their ability to see patterns and relationships. This need to develop the ability to make critical connections between ideas, the need to really understand concepts, and the need to see the value of learning mathematics all can be addressed through an engaging, interdisciplinary approach.

Several things changed as my project developed. First, my original set of research questions reflected the problems I saw with the students I described. So initially, I was interested in looking at understanding and interest in the subject area. After doing research about integrated curricula, I had decided to look at contextualizing the math problems we traditionally did by focusing on the applications to physics. I proposed to our school's curriculum committee that students take physics and calculus simultaneously (most did that already). I also had many conversations with the physics teacher about ways we could work together to integrate the two courses. We envisioned an almost complete integration in some units. During these key units we imagined that we would have essentially one integrated course instead of two distinct courses. The physics teacher and I took a science methods course together over the summer so that we could begin to develop some of our lessons. Those plans all changed when the physics teacher resigned several weeks before the school year began and we hired a new physics teacher. So, instead of the integrated approach to the classes that I had originally imagined, I tried to make the connections between calculus and physics explicit by sequencing the topics in calculus to correspond to the related topics as they were covered in physics.

As we began to plan for an integrated course, I was concerned about maintaining the level of rigor in the approach to the calculus concepts, and my research questions reflected this. My original set of questions also addressed how two teachers would collaborate to achieve the integration we imagined and how I would have to resequence calculus topics to achieve that integration. As I started thinking about what I would actually do in terms of instruction (procedures) and the type of data I could realistically collect, the questions were narrowed to just two.

> Which instructional strategies and learning experiences effectively support an interdisciplinary approach to calculus and physics at the high school level?
>
> What impact does an interdisciplinary approach to calculus and physics at the high school level have on the depth of students' understanding of the concepts?

Jen: Thinking about Thinking

In selecting my research question, a few things influenced my thinking. First of all, I had done some research and a workshop for our staff on metacognition, and have found it to be an interesting topic, and an untapped skill in education. The idea that we have to know how we think and how we work makes so much sense, but if we never ask our students to think about those things, how will these skills ever be developed? A colleague had a quote hanging in her classroom for several years, and it conveys the importance of metacognition: "If we know what we know and how we came to know it, we are powerful people." My colleague was not sure where the quote came from, but even the students in her classes and in mine were able to see the truth in the statement, and in fact, we had an interesting class discussion around the quote in my junior-senior literature class. When I considered the quality of work being produced by the freshmen in the past couple years, I decided that the freshmen should be introduced to these ideas and skills.

It seemed to me—and to many colleagues—that the ninth graders were entering high school with fewer study skills and less self-discipline and self-motivation as compared to ninth graders of eight or ten years ago. The work they turned in was of poor quality, and clearly done at the last minute, rarely proofread, and often not even what the assignment asked for. It seemed to me that these students needed to focus on metacognitive skills as much as—if not more than—their English/reading/writing skills, as these content-related skills would improve with a metacognitive focus.

I had some difficulty choosing this topic because so many people had told me to choose something concrete and finite, a skill that could be taught and measured in a specific chunk of time. However, I kept coming back to the idea of metacognition and my desire to develop the skills of what I now understand to be "self-regulated learning" in my students. I felt that a focus on these skills would make the content of our English classes more relevant and transferable to other classes and to the rest of their lives. It was beginning to become something I felt passionate about, as I had been using various metacognitive skills on a limited basis in my classes, in the form of self-assessments, goal-setting, and revising, and I had seen the value in students developing these skills. However, I felt that they were almost an afterthought, not really part of our everyday routine or language, and so were not becoming automatic skills the students practiced. I decided that I wanted to see what the research would say about teaching specific metacognitive skills, and what would happen in my classroom if I cut out some traditional content to teach these skills.

Because I had done an action research project on a somewhat smaller scale for a class a few years earlier, I had seen the value in doing research this way. It is empowering to be given the opportunity to take a perceived weakness in student performance or achievement and do research on how to improve it and actually try to implement changes for the better, knowing that it does not have to be a perfect, scientific experiment. As a teacher, I know my students, my school, my content area, and it is empowering to be able to make any adjustments I may need to in the implementation of those changes as the "variables" change from week to week, class to class, year to year.
[Note: Jen's final research question was "How is students' ability to monitor and regulate their writing skills and strategies affected by a unit in narrative writing that focuses on metacognition?"]

Sharon: Making It Meaningful

For me, deciding on my research problem was one of the most difficult parts of the research process. Like a lot of professional educators, I have a very wide range of interests, and I'm very much aware of the relevance, importance, and application of so many of my interests to education. As a student in instructional strategies and management techniques, I was required to choose a topic and complete a research project which, I was told, would likely lay the foundation for my master's action research project. The title of my research project for class was "Perceptions, Patterns and Meaningful Learning." While the topic of my action research project, "The Impact of an Intergenerational Friendly Visit Program on Student Perceptions and Attitudes toward Elders and Aging," might seem at first to be an entirely different topic, it is, in fact, just a narrowing down—an application, if you will—of the topic I explored as a student in the strategies class. The funny thing is, though, that I didn't realize until well after completing my action research that these two topics had anything at all to do with each other.

As an educator, I'm constantly exploring and reexploring how it is that the human brain learns. Specifically, I'm intrigued by how experiences over time shape the learner's values and beliefs about himself and his world, and how these resulting attitudes and perceptions color and influence his learning, as well as his participation, involvement, and contributions, both positive and negative, in the community that he is part of.

Like many educators, I entered the field with an idealistic mission to make the world a better place by helping to shape young minds. My specific professional goals from year to year are always in line with my larger, overriding goal of treating each child as the unique and valuable person that he or she is, and creating an environment that encourages positive intra- and interpersonal and academic success, in which learners see themselves as part of the larger community and recognize the responsibility they have to develop their gifts to benefit that community. The purpose of education, I believe, is to prepare young people for effective citizenship in our pluralistic democracy and world community.

Education, I believe, is about *meaningful* learning. Meaningful learning does not occur in a vacuum, but rather, in the context of a given time, place, and culture. In choosing an action research topic, I knew I needed to find something that would reflect this belief and that would be personally meaningful to me, something that wasn't just a rehashing of what I already knew to be true, but something that tested my beliefs and my philosophy of education, and that offered the potential to refine them.

I see education as a microcosm of life. And life is complex and messy. Everything seems to be connected to everything else in some way. So, as

I considered and explored several possible topics, including things like cooperative learning, brain-based learning, emotional intelligence, and so on, I found myself in a hopeless tangle of ideas, each connected to the other and each of equal importance in my mind. Through conversations with colleagues and with my husband, as well as conversations with myself in my head, I realized that I needed to take a deep breath and to let things unfold more authentically. And so I did.

A semester or two before beginning my action research, I worked with gifted and talented (GT) students to produce a play. I was concerned about the elitist attitude I saw among many of these highly able students. This kind of an attitude, I know, is self-defeating and often indicates low self-esteem. And low self-esteem, of course, is linked to underachievement in the school setting, as well as lack of success later in life. I felt that these students needed an authentic, rather than contrived, opportunity to use their time and talent to *really* contribute, not just to horse around and show off. I knew they needed a *real* challenge, an opportunity to *really* learn something and to *really* contribute something. I'm not sure exactly what led me in this direction, but I decided to contact a local nursing home to see about performing our play there. I really honestly can't remember if I read something about service learning, or if my own experiences as a young person came back to tickle my brain, or what. I knew from my own experiences the benefits of authentic learning opportunities through service and interaction with others. I was a caregiver for a cognitively disabled girl for about five years, beginning my freshman year in high school, as well as working as a caregiver for an older disabled man while in college. I also spent time as a trainer in a group home for adult cognitively disabled men. Additionally, my father spent two years in a nursing home before he passed away at the age of fifty-four. All of these people and my experiences with these people challenged my ideas and contributed to the development of my own resiliency and emotional intelligence. Namely, I learned that I have something to offer; I make a difference. Likewise, the people with whom I worked have something to offer too; they each make a difference too. I learned that we're all *smart* and capable in different ways; we all need each other.

These personal life experiences, then, have had a huge impact on my professional values and philosophy of education. Somehow, through the reflective process involved with deciding on a research topic, they surfaced. Performing our play and spending some time with the residents at the nursing home proved to be a challenging and very positive experience for the GT students and me, as well as for the parent chaperones. As I reflected on the ways in which visiting the nursing home impacted all of us, and the interconnected ways this experience *really* reflected my professional values and philosophy of education, I gradually came to see that some type of service learning project would be ideal as an action research topic. As I began doing some initial research, the direction of my project became gradually more focused. Through informal conversations with several people in the field of service learning, as well as through Internet searches and reading, I gradually narrowed my topic down to decide on doing an intergenerational friendly visit program. From there, the tricky part was deciding what aspect of the experience I wanted to evaluate. The answer to that question became more clear only after I was well immersed in the research process.

Looking back on it, deciding on my research topic was both a difficult and extremely valuable experience. I needed to examine and reexamine, organize, refine, consolidate, and actually find words to explain (both to myself and others) what's important to me as an educator. Then I needed to bring all of this together in a research project that would be an authentic extension and application of my educational philosophy. I found this whole process to be at first painfully frustrating and intimidating, and finally hugely, hugely, greatly (sorry, just can't find more sophisticated words here) empowering.

[Note: Sharon's research problem was narrowed to the question, "How can participation in an intergenerational friendly visit program impact children's attitudes and perceptions toward elders and aging?"]

Lenore: Playing to Learn

My research questions were "How does the provision of literacy props enhance student engagement in literacy behaviors?" and "Are play and literacy compatible teaching techniques for kindergarten students? If so, how?" They were selected based upon my need to establish whether or not play truly had a place in early childhood education. At the time of my action research project, education was under tight societal and political scrutiny to enhance educational practices and standards. Play was not seen as a valuable tool in the classroom. Conversely, it was seen by many, including parents and educators in fields other than early childhood education, as a waste of time. It had been my experience that play was a powerful tool for young children to learn, so I decided to see if current research supported my beliefs. If the research supported my educational beliefs, then the research would be useful in educating parents and colleagues. If the research turned out to prove that play was not valuable, then I would have to realign my classroom environment and teaching in order to be a more effective teacher.

I felt very strongly about my action research topic because more and more "first grade" expectations and curriculum with regard to literacy development seemed to be filtering down into kindergarten classrooms. I certainly wanted to provide my students with the best possible learning environment, yet there were varying opinions as to what the "best possible learning environment" was.

CONCLUSION

Each of these teachers chose a project that reflected a passionate concern for children and their needs. Deb decided to integrate physics with calculus because her students were frequently using rote learning to solve math problems. Jen noted a decline in study skills, especially those of planning and goal setting, in incoming freshmen. Sharon wanted to give her students an intergenerational experience that would deepen their empathy and caring for others. Lenore hoped to develop her kindergartners' literacy skills through play.

Finding a problem and turning it into a research question was not an easy process for three of the four teachers. Deb's first idea was to fully integrate calculus and physics. She and her colleague planned together and even took a course to begin lesson planning. However, when the physics teacher left the school, Deb had to revise her plans because the replacement teacher was not open to full integration.

Jen had trouble deciding whether to focus on developing students' metacognitive skills or improving student writing. Of course, she hoped the first would help to accomplish the second. At first she chose to collect data on both. Her friends and colleagues advised her to choose a project that was less complicated. However, her passion for improving students' metacognition overcame any doubt about her choice of topic.

Sharon's interest in a variety of topics made her selection difficult. She finally realized that she needed a topic that was personally meaningful to her, as well as to her students. Her experiences working with mentally retarded children and adults, as well as her experiences caring for her father, had affected her emotional development in powerful ways that she wanted to share with her students.

Perhaps Lenore had an easier time choosing her topic because literacy is a crucial part of the kindergarten experience. She has a strong belief that kindergarteners need developmentally appropriate ways to learn emergent literacy skills. Reacting to the push to make kindergarten more academic, Lenore wanted to know if play was an effective way to engage her students in literacy activities.

While each of these projects was born out of a personal commitment to children, each of the four teachers used educational theory and research to verify that her ideas had merit. Through this process they expanded their understanding of their topics and found ideas to develop their methodologies. Learning to review the research literature is the topic of the next chapter.

3

Reviewing the Literature

Now that you have a research question, you can begin to think about how you are going to answer it. Researchers have asked similar questions, so there is a body of research and theory that you can access to help you think about your question. Looking at the literature related to your topic will help to assure you that your project will have validity, that is, that your findings will be trustworthy. You will learn what other researchers have found regarding your topic. As you read through the literature, you may change or refine your question because you have gained a new or deeper understanding of your topic. In addition, you will be able to ground your project in theoretical and conceptual frameworks. For example, if you want to know how your students are understanding certain science concepts in a problem-based unit, you will need to have a theoretical framework to help you define and operationalize "understanding." (Operationalizing terms will be discussed in the next chapter.) You also may get ideas for useful ways to design your project or collect data. After you have analyzed your data, you will be able to compare your findings with those of other researchers. Your findings may confirm what other researchers have found, or you may need to question why they are different. Figure 3.1 shows the recursive nature of the first part of the action research process.

Your question will determine what subjects need to be researched for your review of literature. You need to pull out the concepts and theoretical and conceptual frameworks in the question. For example, if your

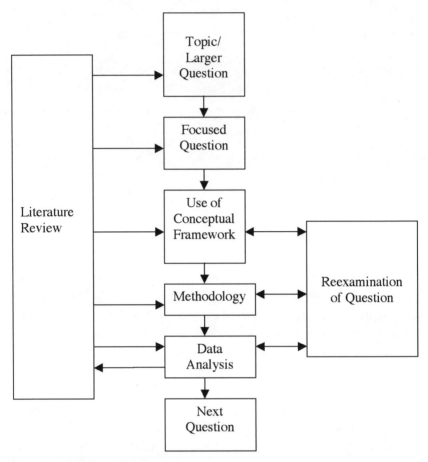

Figure 3.1. Review of Literature

question is "How will participation in an intergenerational program affect the attitudes of fourth graders toward the elderly?" you will need to begin reading about intergenerational programs. You might want to know the following:

- What kinds of intergenerational programs exist?
- What are the purposes of these programs?
- How does one set up an intergenerational program?
- What are the challenges in setting up such a program?
- Have there been any studies that show how young people's attitudes change during an intergenerational program?

Before you design your methodology, you need to know the best thinking and best practices in your area of interest. Why "reinvent the wheel" when there is a rich body of knowledge you can investigate?

What would you need to research if your research question was "What impact does an interdisciplinary approach to math and science have on students' understanding of mathematical concepts?" By looking at the parts of the question, you can determine where to begin researching. In order to answer this question, you should know something about the three parts of the question: interdisciplinary curricula, science and math education, and understanding. You can begin by asking questions about these parts.

- What is the difference between interdisciplinary and integrated curricula?
- How can a teacher design effective interdisciplinary units?
- What do the national math and science standards say about interdisciplinary approaches?
- How will I know whether or not students are understanding the math concepts?
- Is there a model of understanding I can use to assess student learning?

Answering these questions from the research would make a teacher well prepared to design a methodology that would yield valid results.

Exercise A. Look at these research questions. What concepts and frameworks need to be researched?

1. How will cooperative learning affect students' ability to engage in academic discourse in social studies?
2. How will using guided reading help a teacher to meet the needs of individual students?
3. How can a teacher create lessons in language arts that will help students access background knowledge?
4. How can a science teacher use multiple intelligences theory to meet the learning needs of diverse students?
5. How can a teacher design a parent education program to help parents assist their children in reading?

Exercise B. For what topics do you need to do a literature review for your action research project?

WHAT SHOULD I LOOK FOR?

Quality

Before you begin searching, there are a few things you need to know about the literature that's out there. There is a wide range in the quality of books, articles, other action research projects, and websites that you will find. Consider whether you're reading someone's opinion or whether the topic is well researched. Every book, article, or website that you use should have a bibliography or reference list. This list of sources will indicate how well researched the text is. It also will give you suggestions for other sources that you can read. Distinguish between journals that provide teachers with good ideas, like *Mathematics Teacher*, and journals that are research based, like *School Science and Mathematics Journal*. If your action research project involves using project-based learning, you may get a great idea for projects that you could do in an elementary math classroom from *Arithmetic Teacher*, but you should investigate whether project-based learning deepens students' understanding of math concepts before you design your units. In other words, find out whether researchers have established that using projects will accomplish your learning goals and objectives by looking in an academic journal.

Objectivity

Look for books and articles that contradict your position as well as those that support it. If you are researching reading instruction, look at the research on phonics as well as whole language. Ask why whole language replaced direct instruction and why balanced literacy replaced whole language. Seek to understand the historical context of what you are investigating. Look for various viewpoints. Did whole language go out of favor because children weren't learning to read? Was it poorly implemented?

Timeliness

Usually it's best to look at the most current thinking in your field. For some areas it's particularly important that you use recent research. For example, in the field of brain-based learning, scientists are discovering new things about the brain every day. Some theories that were popular, such as the left brain/right brain dichotomy, have been debunked. We now know that the brain can grow new neurons; it wasn't long ago that neuroscientists thought the brain could only grow dendrites. Start by looking at what's been written in the last five years.

Obviously, though, there are cases in which you will want to look at literature that was written several years ago. If your project is dealing with multiple intelligences, you will want to read Howard Gardner's *Frames of Mind* (1983), his seminal work on the topic. However, if you read only this book, you'd be unaware that Gardner has added other intelligences.

Quantity

It's impossible to answer the question "How much should I read?" One clue that you're becoming well read in your field is that you start recognizing names that recur in different bibliographies. When you know who the "big names" in a field are, you can feel confident that you haven't missed any significant information. Do you understand the current trends in the field? Do you understand the historical context of your topic? Have you found research that examines both sides of the issues? Do you have enough information to design a good action research project? If so, you probably can stop researching.

WHERE DO I BEGIN?

The proliferation of online databases and search engines has made searching easier and more accessible for most people. These searching methods, however, are not without their problems. You need to use the correct key or subject words, or you may be searching for hours without results. And if you do find information, you have to be very careful in verifying that it comes from reputable, academic sources. The Internet has lots of treasures but loads of trash, too.

ERIC

You probably want to start your search with the Educational Resources Information Center (ERIC). ERIC was established in 1966 by the United States Department of Education. Although it is very useful, because it is the largest database for education, it is a clearinghouse. This means that it is not refereed like research journals are, so the quality varies greatly.

You can find two kinds of references on ERIC. If the number begins with "ED," it refers to an ERIC document. These documents usually are unpublished studies and reports. They are retrievable using microfiche. Some libraries have complete sets of ERIC microfiche; others can order the documents for you. Some libraries subscribe to EDRS, an online source of "ED" documents. Through these subscriptions, some documents are available free for patrons, or they can be ordered for a fee. Some of these documents are books and can be obtained through your library or interlibrary loan.

Numbers beginning with "EJ" refer to journals. Articles that have been published in professional journals can be located through an ERIC search. Once you have found a title that sounds interesting, check with your library to see if it carries the journal. Otherwise you can get a copy of the article through interlibrary loan. ERIC does provide some full-text articles.

When you begin searching, you will have to determine which keywords will yield the best results. Perhaps you're interested in doing a problem-based unit for your action research project. During a search, 445 entries were found for "problem-based learning." That is too many entries to look at, so you need to limit your search by adding another term. However, only one entry was found for "problem-based learning and K-12 education." There were eleven entries for "problem-based learning and elementary education." Using the correct keyword can make all the difference. There were no entries for "problem-based learning and high school education," but there were 95 entries for "problem-based learning and secondary education." "High school education" is not an ERIC descriptor, so it won't provide any entries.

You can use the Thesaurus of ERIC Descriptors to help determine which terms will yield the best results. ERIC has listed descriptors that capture the main ideas in the thousands of documents that it has catalogued.

By doing a Boolean search, you can use the terms "and," "or," and "not" to broaden your search or narrow it. The keywords "problem-based learning *and* secondary education" told ERIC to search for results that contain both terms. The keywords "problem-based learning *or* secondary education" indicate that each result would contain one of the keywords, but not necessarily both. The keywords "problem-based learning *not* secondary education" would provide results in which the term "problem-based learning" would occur, but not "secondary education."

When you do an ERIC search, the results will be listed from most recent to least recent. Look at the bibliographies in the most recent entries. You will find these bibliographies to be great resources.

AskERIC will answer questions that you have about searching, usually within two working days. E-mail askeric@askeric.org with your questions, and you will receive suggested ERIC and other electronic sources to help you answer them.

Other Databases

Other databases can also be searched, but ERIC is the largest and, therefore, will yield the most results. During one search, ERIC yielded 445 entries for "problem-based learning," Academic Elite had 191, and Middle Search Plus had 8. However, it is good to search more than one database because you may find different results. Databases sometimes provide full texts. However, don't be lured by the ease of using only full-text articles. Find the best sources you can. It is not difficult to order books and articles from other libraries.

Knowing how databases work is important. They generally have some sort of "help" function that can explain this. Databases may look different if you access them from different sources. Different vendors use different procedures and looks, and libraries have some flexibility in customizing databases.

Internet

The Internet can also be searched by using directories or search engines. Directories are generally lists of sites, arranged in hierarchies. You select a category or topic at each level, becoming more and more specific as you search. Yahoo! is an example of a directory. Search engines let you

enter search terms that are searched against indexes of Internet sites. For
most search engines you can use "and," "or," and "not" to limit your
search. AltaVista is an example of a search engine.

Evaluating Internet Sites

The quality of the information on the Internet varies widely. To decide
whether or not a particular site should be used in your review of literature,
consider the following:

- Who is the author? What kind of credentials does this person have?
  Is the person an authority on the topic?
- Is there a bibliography? What are the sources of the information on
  the site? Can you find the same information from other reputable
  sources?
- Why was the information put on the site? Does the person/group have
  an agenda? For example, is the site trying to raise money for a cause?
- Does the site provide multiple perspectives or is the information bi-
  ased?
- How often is the site updated?

Exercise C. Go to the websites listed below. Answer the questions listed
above to determine the credibility and usefulness of these sites. Check if
the sites might be useful for your literature review. (When searching for
websites, you may discover that they have been removed from the Internet. It is possible some of these sites are not available.)

1. http://www.aera.net/
2. http://www.nwrel.org/
3. http://www.msstate.edu/org/msera/msera.html
4. http://www.ncrel.org/ncrel/
5. http://www.ernweb.com/
6. http://www.wcer.wisc.edu/
7. http://ncbe.gwu.edu/tan/randd.htm
8. http://712educators.about.com/mlibrary.htm
9. http://www.nova.edu/ssss/QR/web.html

Books

Books are another valuable resource. If you cannot find a book in your library, you can use interlibrary loan to access books from across the country. *The Handbook of Research on Teaching* (Richardson, 2001) is a gold mine of information. It contains chapters on most curricular areas (e.g., reading, science) that review the latest scholarship in those fields. You can use the bibliographies at the ends of the chapters to find more sources.

TEACHER VOICES

The four teachers, sharing their experiences in action research, now discuss how they approached their reviews of literature and what they learned from their library searches. Their literature reviews sprang from their questions. Deb's question related to using an interdisciplinary approach to using physics applications to develop mathematical understandings. Jen was interested in looking at students' metacognition during a narrative writing unit. Sharon explored children's attitudes toward elders during an intergenerational friendly visit program, and Lenore investigated kindergartners' literacy development while using play. Their stories of engagement, frustration, and achievement will provide inspiration and insight into this rewarding process.

Deb: "One Thing Led to Another"

For the most part, one thing led to another. I started with interdisciplinary curriculum. Actually, I had taken a course on integrating curriculum and that really is where the action research project came from in the first place. I started with the paper I had written for that class and expanded it to include history of the disciplines. I know I then did research on the strategy side. I think that the research on interdisciplinary curriculum led me to Caine and Caine's book, *Making Connections*. Then, in February, we went to David Sousa's workshop on brain-based learning, which fueled that particular fire!

Brain-based led me to constructivism. Brooks and Brooks, in *In Search of Understanding: The Case for Constructivist Classrooms,* also talked about understanding, and the whole [constructivist] philosophy challenged the traditional style of assessment. I was also concerned about assessment because I was aware of the need to triangulate data and so was looking for ways to assess understanding beyond just looking at test scores. Research on constructivism also led to investigating strategies like project- and problem-based learning, which I didn't use directly, but did focus on the importance of giving problems a real-world context. Physics was the context for calculus. I also researched modeling because of its connection to problem-based learning and because it was the approach the physics teacher used. National Council of Teachers of Mathematics (NCTM) Standards–based education also emphasized things like alternate assessment, nontraditional classroom approaches, problem solving, reasoning, and communication—all of which was consistent with brain-based and constructivist theories.

Metacognition was actually the last thing I considered. Like assessment, it emerged from a need to actually generate and triangulate data. I did several things specifically to get the students to "make their thinking visible" in order to collect data. I had them respond to prompts about understanding a topic; videotaped presentations; interviewed them individually, in pairs, and in small groups; asked them to write about problems. In the interviews particularly, I asked them directly how studying calculus impacted their study of physics and vice versa. It became apparent that these conversations and presentations and writing assignments were actually promoting understanding, not just "measuring" it. That's when I went back and looked at metacognition and its impact on learning.

Jen: "On the Right Track"

For my review of literature, I first researched metacognition—particularly in education, because there have been, and there continue to be, so many definitions of the term. This required some synthesis of information, because there was quite a bit of overlap, but it was interesting to see all the different studies that have been done about the topic. I chose this topic because I had done some brief research on it for a previous class, and because a colleague had been using it with success in her classroom. So, I thought it would be a good idea for my topic, so I could see what researchers have found and then implement some of those ideas with my own students. I did not find a single study that concluded that metacognition is not beneficial for students. The research process was, in fact, very encouraging, because research showed that some course content would have to be sacrificed in order to include metacognitive skills, and this was a concern of mine—how to "fit" everything in. I learned that this was an acceptable "sacrifice," because of the greater benefits of metacognition, benefits that would transcend my individual classroom. This "less is more" thinking began to make sense to me, because, of course, we cannot teach students everything there is to know in our discipline, so wouldn't it be better to teach them metacognitive skills that they could then use in *any* learning situation, so that they can learn some content on their own? My attitudes and methodology began to shift from the belief that my job was to teach students "English" to the belief that my job is to teach students *how* to learn, and show what they know, and that "English" is simply one way of doing that.

I also researched teaching writing and focusing on narration. I chose these topics because our department was working on developing a narrative writing unit for our ninth graders. The connections I found were again encouraging. It seemed we were on the right track. Experts asserted that using narrative writing is best for developing writers because it focuses on the self, as metacognition does. This gave credibility to our departments' philosophy about teaching writing to the ninth graders and opened the door for me to try new methodologies with the students. It was a bit of an "A-ha!" because it made so much sense to put these things together, but I had never stopped to think about it before. I used several techniques from the research I did and adapted them to fit my particular class and students. As I've said before, this was an empowering process, because I had research to support my questions and methodologies, and I had access to some effective practices—instructional and assessment practices—that I could try in my own class, so I didn't feel as if I were "reinventing the wheel." In terms of the research on teaching writing, I was relieved to see similar concerns [to the ones] I had, particularly regarding student peer assessment; I had not had much luck with it, and some research suggested that it is not an effective practice, so I felt supported in my concerns, and I was relieved to have some research to back up my reasons for cutting back on peer assessment, in favor of more ongoing self-assessment and teacher assessment.

The research process, while difficult at times, was invaluable in shaping my attitudes and methodologies, not only in the course that was the focus for my study, but in all my courses.

Sharon: "Nothing Less than Life Changing"

The process that I went through in initiating this project on intergenerational programming, and learning how to let go enough to let it evolve in this continuous and sort of fluid way, was nothing less than life changing. Specifically, with regard to the review of literature, my feelings moved from being overwhelmed and frustrated, to humbled, and finally on to empowered. I had, after all, in the end, achieved what seemed to me to be, at first, a completely undoable goal.

As I sifted through my humongous pile of resources, a number of things began to happen. First of all, I little by little began to develop a working knowledge of the vocabulary I needed to speak effectively and to search effectively to get answers to my questions. Conversely, what I was reading and hearing from people began to make more sense. Secondly, I began to create in my head a sort of map or mental image of what I could now refer to as the intergenerational field. I began to understand that the intergenerational field, at the time, was only currently evolving into its own discipline and that resources, therefore, might be tricky to find; not a lot of old tried and true reading to do, but rather, I'd need to focus on very current research and do some detective work to see how this body of knowledge supports or is related to the cornerstone work of educational theorists like Piaget and Vygotsky. I also realized that, due to the fact that intergenerational programming as its own field was in its infancy, a logical place to look for information would be to contact current researchers and practitioners, which I did. Here is where I found my gold mine. Each contact led to other contacts and to other resources. People in this field, I found, are passionate about what they do. These people inspired and encouraged me and shared resources and ideas with me. I discovered the beauty of the Internet, which was an invaluable source of information for me, once I knew what to look for (what names to look for, what vocabulary to use, etc.). And, finally, as I read and listened and talked to people, and as I reflected on my personal philosophy of education, all of the ideas that, in the beginning, were just a big old messy tangle of confusion, sort of smoothed themselves out, and I came up with a research question that made sense; it was doable and it was important.

My methodology came directly from my work in the review of literature. Research indicated what type of methodology made sense, and I followed these guidelines to create a research-based chronology and methodology of lessons, experiences, and assessment/evaluation tools.

My work in the review of literature was really a multifaceted, evolving process of struggle, discovery, reflection, and metacognition—revisiting ideas and moving on, going back to revisit and moving on, shaping and reshaping. In the end I felt an enormous sense of ownership and investment in my project; I had really created it, it really was mine.

What I learned is that I'm a capable person. Believing, really believing that I'm capable makes me capable. We need to give students the opportunity to really, authentically succeed. These kinds of statements are overused, so much so that I think people don't really *hear* them anymore. But I don't know what other words to use to say what I mean. In education, the single biggest job we have is to teach in such a way that we hold up a mirror to students—not just some students, but all students—so that they can see their capable self. It's amazing, just *really* amazing, what can be accomplished by someone who feels capable.

Lenore

I researched literature in the following four main areas: the value of play, developmentally appropriate practice, literacy development, and the integration of literacy and play.

I chose to research the value of play because I needed to find out what the latest research had to offer regarding play. It was important to know whether or not play truly had educational value. Did the research support play within a classroom setting? I discovered that the research supported play as an effective learning tool for young children. My research led me to review familiar names in education, such as Piaget and Vygotsky. It also led me to very specific and practical studies on designing effective kindergarten classroom settings for play, as well as guidelines for teacher observations and interactions with students during play. The studies that focused specifically on kindergarten classrooms were especially useful with the methodology portion of my project.

I researched developmentally appropriate practice (DAP) because it has been the cornerstone of early childhood education since the late 1980s. DAP offers an understanding of how young children learn. It gives guidelines for promoting the best possible educational environment. The research of developmentally appropriate practice gave me a deeper understanding of what it actually is, and what it is not. The information I acquired researching DAP gave me a stronger foundation and deeper understanding of my teaching practices. That was, and continues to be, extremely helpful in allowing me to educate parents about appropriate educational practices for young children.

Literacy development was a crucial part of research for this project. Exactly how did young children develop literacy skills? Were there literacy practices that encouraged, fostered, and sustained literacy development in young children? My research in the area of literacy development led me to numerous historical practices and perspectives. What struck me the most was how various practices have surfaced, disappeared, and resurfaced (usually with a different name) over time. I read numerous perspectives on literacy development. I ultimately discovered that a balance between child-initiated activities and teacher-directed activities seemed to be the most effective method of literacy development in early childhood classrooms.

Finally, I needed to see if research had linked literacy development and play. Were these two aspects of development truly compatible? Could play environments be set up to foster literacy development in young children? This particular area of research turned out to be the most powerful research I did with regard to enhancing my teaching abilities. The research demonstrated a strong and positive connection between literacy and play in early childhood classrooms. It gave me specific strategies to implement and, once again, information that I could share with parents to help them understand and support my classroom practices.

CONCLUSION

These teachers became experts in their topics by doing their literature reviews. They not only developed content knowledge but also learned about various methodologies as they gained confidence as teachers and researchers. Deb discovered various ways to collect data that promoted student understanding, as well as ways to measure and describe it. As one topic led to another, Deb developed a love for scholarly work. Jen tackled profound questions about her role as a teacher and concluded that she needed to teach students how to learn instead of only focusing on her subject, English. She also felt a sense of empowerment when she found research that supported her belief that the ninth-grade writing curriculum should begin with narrative writing, and when she realized that narrative writing and metacognition meshed because of the focus on self. Sharon's review of literature helped her to refine her research question and find an appropriate methodology; she was deeply affected by her sense of accomplishment and the realization of her own capabilities. Lenore looked at using play to develop literacy skills to assure herself that she would be developing a literacy program that was theoretically sound and developmentally appropriate.

Each of these teachers found that looking at scholarly research and theory can be confusing, frustrating, and messy at times, but it is ultimately rewarding. In later chapters you will see how their literature reviews deeply affected their attempts to ensure validity in their studies.

It is common to be overwhelmed, at first, by the amount of material that is available. Try to find out who the leading scholars in the field are. Look at who they cite and who cites them. As you become an expert on your topics, you will gain the confidence to proceed with your implementation.

4

Designing the Methodology

Now that you have thought about your question(s) and researched the literature that relates to your topic(s), you need to think about how you're going to conduct your study. Previous chapters have discussed the importance of the research question and the usefulness of the review of literature in ensuring validity in your study. This chapter will discuss other key aspects of validity.

Before we discuss the specifics of your study, it might be useful to look at some research designs. While you will not be using any of these designs, they do raise some issues that you too will need to address in developing your project.

QUANTITATIVE DESIGNS

Quantitative research measures the extent to which or how well something is done. It seeks only answers that can be quantified. Validity is addressed in the design of the methodology and the analysis of the data. Researchers strive to make sure that they are reporting relationships that really exist. Internal validity refers to the credibility of the conclusions drawn from the data regarding the effectiveness of the treatment. External validity pertains to the generalizability of these effects to other groups.

Here are some examples of quantitative designs. Each has different strengths and weaknesses in ensuring validity. The following definitions

are taken from *How to Design and Evaluate Research in Education*
(Fraenkel and Wallen, 2003).

Exercise A. Read the following explanations and examples. Answer the
question after each example.

1. Experimental—an independent (experimental) variable is manipulated
   while other variables are controlled; the effect on the dependent variable is observed; this is one of a few designs that can show causality.

   To control for confounding variables, researchers use random
   samples (every member of the population has an equal chance of being selected for the study) and random assignment (individuals are
   assigned randomly to the experimental and control groups). Sometimes a stratified random sample (subgroups are represented in the
   sample in the same proportion as in the population) is used. For example, we know that race and class can have an impact on achievement. If you were studying the effects of a certain reading program
   on reading achievement, you'd have to make sure that your two
   groups were equivalent in terms of race and class. There may be
   other factors that affect reading achievement. What if one group had
   a significantly larger number of boys than girls in it? Gender could
   also be a confounding variable. One of the researchers' main concerns is that significant, extraneous variables are equally distributed
   in both groups. In other words they need to know whether or not the
   experimental variable is causing the effect, rather than some other
   variable.

   Example—Suppose you want to know whether mentoring improves students' attendance in high school. You could select all the
   ninth graders in a high school with low attendance. You could randomly select fifty of those students and randomly assign them to two
   groups: twenty-five would receive mentoring and twenty-five would
   not. At the end of the study, students' attendance would be compared.
   • Would you want to use a stratified random sample? Why or why not?
2. Causal-comparative—an attempt to discover the cause for or the
   consequences of existing conditions in groups or individuals. Some-

times researchers want to know the effect of a certain variable, for example gender, on achievement. Studies have shown that girls usually perform better in language activities and boys in mathematical ones. Causal-comparative studies attempt to suggest causation, but causation can be proved only with experimental designs.

Example—Suppose you have a group with an existing condition, for instance, gender, and you want to know whether females have a greater ability to do spatial reasoning. You could look at a group of males and a group of females and measure their ability in spatial reasoning.

• Do you see any weaknesses in this design?

3. Correlational—examination of two variables to see if a relationship exists; it is used to predict what will happen to one variable if the other increases or decreases; it does not show causality. In correlational research, one needs two variables that can be quantified (not categorical variables, like gender). Early lawsuits against tobacco companies, claiming that smoking caused lung cancer, were not successful because correlations could show that there was a positive relationship between smoking and deaths from lung cancer, but could not prove causality. Could there have been other causes, like genetic predispositions, sedentary lifestyles, or air pollution? One must be able to make a convincing argument, using logic and a preponderance of evidence, that correlations do strongly suggest that causality exists. Juries were eventually convinced by these arguments and ruled against tobacco companies.

Example—Suppose you wanted to know whether there was a relationship between the amount of disruptive behavior in a classroom and the teacher's expectation of failure. You could measure each variable and see whether there is a positive correlation (as one increases, so does the other) or a negative correlation (as one increases, the other decreases) or no correlation at all.

• How could a researcher quantify "teacher's expectations of failure"? What do you think the research would show?

4. Survey—an attempt to discover a certain group's status with regard to certain variables. Information is gathered about people's opinions,

attitudes, knowledge, and so on. Many problems affect the trustworthiness of the survey results. The instrument may be confusing or misleading. Those surveyed may not represent the larger population, or the sample size may not be large enough. The researcher may get a poor response rate.

Example—Perhaps you want to know about your students' study habits at home. You could survey the parents.

• What problems in analyzing the survey results could occur? What other group could you survey to corroborate the results?

QUALITATIVE DESIGNS

Qualitative research seeks to describe the quality of certain aspects of a phenomenon. Instead of trying to quantify certain effects, relationships, or attitudes, qualitative researchers seek to understand how or why something is done. They examine complex situations in great depth.

Validity in qualitative research is a complex and contentious issue. Some researchers have eschewed the term because of its origin in quantitative research and substituted "trustworthiness" (Zeichner and Noffke, 2001). Theories of validity in qualitative research range from that of Lincoln and Guba (1985), who call for new criteria for validity, to that of Goetz and LeCompte (1984), who use the quantitative terms "internal validity" and "external validity," but modify the meanings to fit qualitative research. Some terrorists use the term "truth value" to refer to the confidence in the truthfulness of the findings, "applicability" to refer to the degree to which these findings can be applied to other contexts, "consistency" to refer to the ability to reproduce the same findings in similar contexts, and "neutrality" to refer to the degree to which the findings are free of researcher bias (Guba and Lincoln, 1981, p. 103). These terms convey the same concerns as the scientific paradigm's use of "internal validity for truth value, external validity or generalizability for applicability, reliability for consistency, and objectivity for neutrality" (p. 104).

Qualitative research has many variations. Listed below are just a few. There is overlap in the following definitions. "Ethnographic" and "naturalistic" can be used interchangeably. Many ethnographers use participant observation. These definitions are taken from *How to Design and Evaluate Research in Education* (Fraenkel and Wallen, 2003).

5. Ethnographic—the collection of data on many variables in a naturalistic setting to gain a holistic understanding of a particular group in a particular culture. Ethnographers work to interpret the culture of a group by spending long periods of time in the setting, by understanding multiple perspectives and the larger contexts of various issues, and by reporting their findings in thick, rich description.

   Example—You might want to know the effect of a new principal on a school during the first year of her tenure. You would visit the school frequently; interview the administrators, students, staff, parents; attend meetings; collect artifacts; as well as collect other data to give a complete picture of the effect of the principal on the school.

   • What kinds of difficulty might this study present?

6. Naturalistic—the collection of data while the researcher controls nothing and does not affect the observed in any way. The researcher tries to be as unobtrusive as possible as she observes the individuals in their natural setting.

   Example—If you wanted to understand how girls and boys interact while playing during recess, you could watch them from a distance and note their interactions.

   • Would there be any ethical dilemmas for the researcher?

7. Participant observer—an outside researcher becomes a participant in the research. Sometimes the researcher makes her presence known to the members of the group as she works with them while observing them and collecting data. Other times researchers remain "undercover" to get more accurate data. However, the ethics of observing people without their knowledge is questionable.

   Example—You might want to study how teachers work together to create interdisciplinary units. You would join a group of teachers in writing a curriculum and observe them, take notes, interview them, collect artifacts, and then analyze and describe their interactions.

   • What problems with objectivity might the researcher have?

8. Case study—in-depth investigation of individuals or groups used to determine the relationship between certain variables and certain behaviors.

   Example—You might have two students in your class, one who understands math concepts very quickly and one who struggles. You might study the two students over the course of the year to try and determine what is contributing to the difference.
   • Would you be able to generalize to other students who are having difficulty in math?

9. Content Analysis—analysis of written or visual contents of a document. This kind of analysis can yield interesting information about a group within a culture indirectly by examining its beliefs and behaviors through its communications. To do a content analysis, you must clarify what you are analyzing by defining the terms and deciding what you will look at, then create a sampling plan. You need to choose categories that you will use to examine the content. Indirect study of this kind can supplement other research methods, such as surveys or participant observation. One drawback to this kind of analysis is that the content must be in a written or recorded form. Interpretation of content analysis also presents problems. The quality of the content analysis will depend in part upon the degree to which the categories of analysis match the intended meaning of what is being studied.

   Example—If you wanted to analyze the treatment of women in a literature textbook, you would define what you meant by "treatment of women characters" and create categories that you could use in your analysis. You might look at how these characters are described physically, psychologically, and spiritually.
   • What other topics could you look at in a literature textbook?

DESIGN OF YOUR STUDY

As you design your action research study, you need to think about the setting, the participants, the procedures, the data collection methods, and finally data analysis.

By doing the following exercises, you should be able to outline your methodology.

Setting

Where you do your study will have a great impact on your results. Schools across the United States have different cultures. They have different expectations, standards, curricula, teachers, students, and parents. You may be in a small rural school or a large urban school. When other teachers read your action research study, they may want to implement your methodology in their classrooms. They won't be able to generalize your results; however, they may think your schools are similar enough that your project could be implemented in their schools. Or they may realize your school is very different from theirs and make some modifications to the project to create a better fit for their students. Describing your school and students in detail is a way to deal with issues of external validity, that is, applicability to other contexts.

What is important about your setting? How is it like and different from other schools?

Exercise B. Answer the following questions. Describe the attributes that best characterize your district and school.

1. Describe your district, if you are in a school district (urban or rural, size, socioeconomic status [SES], etc.).
2. Describe your school (private or public, size, grades, ethnicity, location, management style, specialty, etc.).

Participants

The results of your study will vary, depending on your students. Teachers know that one class can be vastly different from another. Students can behave differently in the morning than in the afternoon. Students have individual needs and learning styles. Gender, race, and class can have an impact on how students learn. These variables are just a few of those that have an impact on learning.

Most elementary teachers will be working with one class of students throughout the day. Therefore, they won't be choosing which students will be participants in their study unless they are selecting a few students for case studies. Most secondary teachers work with more than one class each day. They will have to choose which class to use for their studies.

If you need to select one class, choose the most representative class, unless you have a reason not to. For example, you might want to work with a low-achieving group on study skills. In most cases, however, you want to choose your most typical class. Don't choose the first class of the day if they are sleepy in the morning, and don't choose the last class of the day if they are extremely energetic.

Limit your participants to one class. You will be collecting a great deal of data, so you don't want to be overwhelmed with data from two or more classes. In most cases, you should not try to compare two classes. If you want to use one method with one class and one with another, how will you know that it was the method that made a difference rather than some other variable, like ability, time of day, or special needs?

Consider using case studies and looking at a few students in depth. Case studies are not appropriate for all projects. But perhaps you are beginning to use guided reading with your first graders, and you want to know how effective it is for meeting the needs of diverse learners. You could assess the reading levels of your class and choose two students who aren't reading yet, two who are reading on grade level, and two who are reading above grade level. Although you'd be assessing the reading progress of all your students throughout the year, for the study you'd be collecting more data on these six students during a limited amount of time.

You are also a participant in your study. In quantitative research, the researcher should be transparent and not influence the study in any way. In action research you are studying yourself, your students, and your classroom. You are intrinsically involved in the study. You will try to remain as objective as possible when collecting data—for instance, by examining student work—and when drawing conclusions; however, you bring your own beliefs, biases, values, skills, knowledge, and personality to your classroom and to your action research.

Exercise C. Who will participate in your study?

1. Describe your class (age, gender, special needs, ethnicity, etc.).
2. How did you select this group of students? (Answer if you have more than one class to choose from.)

3. Describe yourself as the teacher-researcher. Do you have any special training in your topic?

Procedures

What are you going to do during your study? Your procedures are the heart of your study, and you need to think about them very carefully.

Think about what you learned from your review of literature. What have you learned that will inform your methodology? Let's say you investigated using brain-based learning because you want to incorporate some of these strategies into your classroom. You have asked the question, "How can a teacher use brain-based learning principles to affect students' understanding of fractions?" You might want to consider the following:

If the brain is a social brain, then you need to include more opportunities for students to engage in meaningful discourse.

If students construct their own knowledge, then you need to give them opportunities to observe and hypothesize—to use inductive thinking.

If assessment and instruction are cyclic, then you need to give more frequent and explicit feedback to students throughout the learning process.

Then you can start thinking about designing a unit that will have those components: opportunities for writing and talking about fractions, the use of manipulatives to allow observing and hypothesizing, and a process of increasing your feedback to students.

You also need to think about the length of time your study will require. If your study involves teaching a unit on fractions, your study will be in the same time period as the unit. However, what if your study deals with the use of guided reading? You'll be using guided reading for the entire year. Then you have to think about how long you will collect data. Your study has to be long enough to see some growth in student achievement, but it shouldn't be so long that you are overwhelmed with data.

Exercise D. Map your question and procedures by using some sort of visual organizer, like figure 4.1.

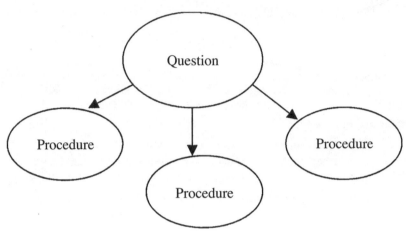

Figure 4.1.   Visual Organizer

Think about what you have learned from the mapping and what impli-cations this learning has for your methodology. Answer the following questions.

1. How did you design your study? Did you use any research?
2. What activities are you going to do with your students? (Develop your map into a plan.)
3. What resources will you use (books, speakers, field trips, etc.)?
4. Are you designing any materials? If so, what kind?
5. What is your timeline?

Data Collection

How are you going to collect your data? You need to triangulate your data, that is, you need to collect data from at least three sources. This kind of data collection helps to ensure validity because you will be making infer-ences from multiple sources rather than drawing on one source to form a conclusion.

There are many sources that you can use to collect your data. Before you decide, you need to do a few things. Look at your question(s) again. What terms need to be defined? What terms need to be opera-tionalized? In other words, you need to determine what something looks and sounds like before you can decide what data to collect. For example, if you want to examine the impact of teaching social skills on group interactions, what are you going to see and hear when a student is collaborating?

Use the following criteria to operationalize concepts.

1. Can you see or hear it?
2. Can you state it positively?
3. Is observing it feasible?

Here is how collaboration might be operationalized.
Student is

- facing other students
- making eye contact with other students
- sharing ideas
- asking for elaboration
- asking appropriate questions
- sharing materials

Exercise E. Operationalize one of the following:

a. Interest in reading
b. Tolerance toward people from different cultures
c. Empathy toward others

Operationalize the concepts in your question.

Now review your research question and procedures as you read the following section. Think about which of the following data collection methods would be appropriate for your question.

Journal

Every teacher-researcher must keep a daily journal. It is the most important way that you will have to keep track of the details of your study. Record objective notes about what is happening in your classroom.

Also include your reflections on what is happening. Ask yourself the following questions: What does this mean? Why do I think it is significant? Do I need to change something? Does it connect to something else? Do I see any patterns emerging? Can I draw any preliminary conclusions?

Although it will be a struggle to find time each day to write in your journal, your efforts will pay off when you analyze your data. You will have a detailed, accurate record of your project rather than a jumble of half-forgotten memories.

One way you can include both kinds of information is to use one page for objective observations and the opposing page for reflections. Figure 4.2 provides an example.

Exercise F. Describe an event that occurred in your class. Write objective observations and reflective comments about this event.

Student Work

Student work is one of the most valuable ways to gain insights into student learning. You can collect written work, quizzes, and tests. You may want to photograph some of it. Lessons can be videotaped and audiotaped. A portfolio may be helpful to organize student work.

A Candidate's Guide to NBC 2001–02 offers suggestions for analyzing student work for teachers working on National Board Certification. Here are twelve questions that may be helpful in looking at the work of your students.

Objective Observations	Reflective Comments
10–28 students brainstormed ideas for paper together. 9 of 24 students participated.	Most students seemed to enjoy the activity. Next time I'll let them brainstorm individually and then share suggestions with the class.

Figure 4.2.   Objective Observations and Reflective Comments

1. What was the learning goals(s) of this assignment?
2. How does this work assignment demonstrate the learning goal(s)?
3. What did the student understand about the concept?
4. What did the student misunderstand about the concept?
5. What patterns of errors are evident in the work?
6. What criteria did I use to assess this work sample? (Not how did I grade the paper!)
7. How did the student assess his/her own work?
8. How did I give the student constructive feedback?
9. How is the feedback evident to the assessors?
10. What do I need to explain or reteach about this concept?
11. Based on the analysis of this work sample, what does the student need to learn next?
12. How can I connect future instruction to this learning? (American Federation of Teachers and National Education Association, 2001–2, p. 21)

By answering some or all of these questions, you may gain valuable insights into how your students are learning, what misunderstandings are blocking the learning, and how your instruction and assessment practices are influencing the learning.

You may want to develop a rubric to assess student work and check for progress.

Rubrics

Rubrics are scoring guides that delineate the criteria and the gradations of quality for student work. "What elements must the work contain?" and "How well must these be completed for a certain grade or score?" are two questions that will help you to develop your rubric. Before designing your rubric, look at sample rubrics for ideas. When writing your rubric, use clear, specific language to capture observable qualities. For example, don't use the phrase, "has an interesting introduction" or "has a boring introduction" to describe an element in a composition. "Interesting" and "boring" are too subjective. Instead think about the strategies a writer might use to capture the readers' attention, for example, using an anecdote or questions, and be more objective and specific in describing the degrees of quality in the introduction. You will need to put a great deal of thought into your rubric. However, if you have a well-designed rubric, it should be fairly easy to use.

Videotaping and Audiotaping

Videotaping and audiotaping provide useful ways to capture a lesson. You may want to videotape and/or audiotape your students before you begin the study so that they will become used to it. Some students will act silly if they aren't used to being taped. Videotapes and audiotapes can be transcribed so that you have a written version to analyze. Make sure you get parental permission and check the policy in your school district.

Checklists

Once you've operationalized your terms, you can turn them into a checklist of observable behaviors. For example, as students collaborate in groups, you can check off that they are facing each other or making eye contact. For example:

Collaboration
Student is
___ facing other students
___ making eye contact with other students
___ sharing ideas
___ asking for elaboration
___ asking appropriate questions
___ sharing materials

Keep the number of items on the checklist manageable, so you can easily circulate around the room and check off the items.

Surveys

Fraenkel and Wallen (1990) have offered suggestions for using surveys. Think about whether you want open-ended or closed questions. Open-ended questions will yield richer data, but those data will be more diffi-cult to analyze. Closed questions are easier to tabulate. Both kinds of questions are subject to misinterpretation, so they must be worded care-fully. You can use both types of questions on your survey.

Some suggestions for writing closed questions are as follows:

1. Avoid ambiguity. Make the questions clear.
2. Focus each question on only one thought.
3. Make the questions short.
4. Keep the language simple; avoid jargon.
5. Don't use language that would bias the respondent.
6. Don't use leading questions.
7. Don't use double negatives. (pp. 338–340)

Some surveys use a Likert scale to quantify responses to closed questions. These questions start with a statement that must be reacted to with choices like "always," "usually," "occasionally," and "never." Numerical values are assigned to the answers: always = 4, usually = 3, occasionally = 2, never = 1. For example, you could state, "After I've read a story, I think about the meaning of the title." The higher the response the more likely a stu-dent is to consider the meaning of a title after reading a story. You could sur-vey your class and get a mean score to determine the likelihood of students reflecting on a title (Mills, 2000).

Make sure you maintain the anonymity of those taking your survey. If you are giving the survey to students, provide a quiet setting. Students should not talk to each other while they are taking the survey.

Before you give the survey, proofread it carefully and make sure it is at-tractive. Don't make it too long.

Exercise G. Rewrite these survey questions so that they meet Fraenkel and Wallen's criteria. Explain what the problems are in each question.

1. Do you spend a lot of time reading?
2. Do you like to read books about real men and women who have ac-complished great things, or do you like to read about fictional char-acters?
3. How does asking predicting questions help you to better compre-hend the story?

4. Would you not be interested in reading books about people from other cultures?
5. Why do you think reading is important?

Interviews

While interviews take more time than surveys, they often provide detailed responses that surveys don't. You can establish rapport with your interviewee and perhaps get information that would not be shared on a survey. You can ask the person to expand on an answer or clarify it. Consider taping your interview if the interviewee is not uncomfortable with the tape recorder.

Some of the same suggestions that were mentioned for surveys apply to interviews. Carefully word your questions. Make them clear and keep the language simple. Choose a location that provides privacy for you and the interviewee.

Pre- and Posttests

Depending on your question(s), it may be appropriate to give students a test before and after the study so that you can see any changes in achievement. The tests could be objective. Depending upon your study, you could also use a writing sample that is assessed for various characteristics. You might want to give students an essay prompt before the study begins and give the same prompt at the end of the study to compare the changes that have occurred in student writing.

Making Connections

Your data collection methods must be able to provide data with which you can answer your research question. You need to think about the kinds of data each method will provide. While reading the previous section, you may have found methods that will work for your question. Perhaps you discovered a method in your literature review. Whatever methods you use, they must match your question and your procedures.

Here's an example of an action research project that I conducted in my English 10 class when I was teaching in a large, urban high school. Notice the connections among all the parts of the research process.

My research question was "In what ways can students' use of a metaphor strategy influence their engagement in reading poetry?" In my review of literature I couldn't find a strategy for understanding metaphor, so I needed to investigate the research on metaphors. I also needed to know about strategy instruction and engagement in reading. I needed to know how I would recognize whether or not students were engaged in reading. Then I designed my methodology. A metaphor strategy had to be created. A metaphor unit had to be developed and taught.

For my data collection I did the following. By using Rosenblatt's (1978) notion of active reading and Wang and Palincsar's (1989) concept of active learning, I defined engagement in reading as having three qualities: 1) an openness to the text; 2) an openness to one's personal experiences, attitudes, and prior knowledge; and 3) persistence. Therefore, I had to find ways to capture the degree to which the students were engaged in these three aspects of engagement. In terms of collecting data, I kept reflective and descriptive field notes in a journal to create a daily record of the activities in the class. I collected all student written work. I videotaped the lessons and transcribed the discussions so that I had a written text to analyze. I had students do a pre- and postwriting sample, discussing an extended metaphor in a poem. Two readers assessed the students' essays, looking for changes in the students' ability to analyze the use of metaphor. From these multiple sources, I was able to draw some conclusions about how my students progressed in their ability to analyze metaphors by persistently bringing their own backgrounds to the text while paying close attention to it.

Exercise H. What if your research question were the following: How can the use of problem-based learning impact students' understanding of Newton's laws of motion?

1. What would you have to research for the review of literature?
2. What would you have to consider in order to design the methodology?
3. What data could you collect?
4. Review your question, procedures, and data collection methods. Are they tightly connected?

In order to match data collection methods to your research question, you need to think about what kind of information each data collection method yields.

Method	Information
Journal	
Student Work	
Video and Audiotapes	
Checklists	
Surveys	
Interviews	
Pre- and Post-tests	
Other	
Other	

Figure 4.3.   Methods and Information

Exercise I. Use figure 4.3 to record the kinds of information about learning that each method can provide.

Now that you've considered various kinds of data collection methods, you can decide which of these will supply the most useful data for your study. Remember that you need at least three to triangulate your data.

Exercise J. Answer the following questions.

1. What other data collection methods could you use in addition to the ones in the chart?
2. Which ones will you use in your study? (Choose at least three.) Why did you choose these methods?
3. What will happen to the data after the study? Will you give them back to students or will you destroy them?

Confidentiality and Anonymity

All of your data should remain confidential. You need to assure parents that you are protecting the rights of their children. Most times you will not be able to ensure anonymity, because students will put their names on their work. If you are using a survey, it can be anonymous to encourage more honesty in the responses.

Exercise K. Answer the following question.

1. How will you ensure confidentiality and anonymity?

TEACHER VOICES

The four teachers again share their stories, talking now about how they designed their projects and collected their data. Notice that their procedures came from their questions, that they used their literature reviews to design their methodologies, and that they triangulated their data.

Deb: Integrating for Understanding

As part of the research I did in my review of literature, I looked at Robin Fogarty's models for integrated curriculum. What I was trying to do by connecting calculus and physics seemed to draw some elements from each of three models: sequenced, shared, and threaded. I resequenced some calculus topics so that what I was teaching in calculus would be timed to match what was being taught in physics. By collaborating, to a degree, with the physics teacher, we identified things like vocabulary and notation that the two courses shared. I also looked at instructional strategies used in physics and included or threaded the same type of learning activities throughout calculus.

To outline my methodology, I thought in terms of process and content integration. As soon as the year began, I started using process strategies that were similar to those used in physics. For example, the Calculus Consortium based at Harvard University promoted what was called the rule of three: the use of numeric (tables of values), graphic, and algebraic approaches to problems. The students extensively used the Texas Instruments graphing calculator to explore and solve problems. In physics, students were using modeling to generate data and using graphical analysis software to analyze them. As a result, students were given opportunities to develop skills in the use of technology. The technology made very abstract ideas like equations concrete and visual by graphing them, and students were forced to be able to shift from one representational form (numeric, algebraic, graphic) to the others.

Another process element was communication. This, too, was supported by the Harvard project as well as NCTM. Communication in both classes was both oral and written. Students were given prompts to respond to or questions to answer in writing. In class, students regularly collaborated to solve problems and then presented their results.

Collaboration was very important in both classes. NCTM emphasizes the value of "discourse," and collaboration provided an arena for verbal communication.

The first area of content integration involved vocabulary and notation. The physics teacher and I coordinated our use of simple terms like "independent" and "dependent variable" as well as more technically complex terms like "negative acceleration." Mathematical notation was adjusted to match the notation in physics and to make expressions more meaningful — like the use of the variable t to represent time. The hope was that the consistent use of terminology and notation would help students make connections between the two subjects.

One of the most important steps in implementing the integration was timing the introduction of topics to match what was going on in physics. This required a great deal of interaction with the physics teacher.

The most important move in terms of resequencing the calculus topics involved moving the study of antiderivatives to a time much earlier in the course than it would be in a traditional sequence. The antiderivative of simple functions was presented along with the process of finding the derivatives. Since the two processes are opposites (like addition and subtraction), there was a logical connection. This one alteration opened up a variety of applications in physics that would not have been possible without it. And, like material covered earlier in the course, relationships were viewed from numeric, algebraic, and graphic perspectives.

Data Collection

Throughout the course of the project, I kept a journal where I would record questions students would ask or descriptions of discussions I had observed. Most of the information I recorded I had observed directly, but I also made note of observations the physics teacher shared with me. Student work was also part of the data I collected. This included not just the mathematical process they had recorded, but also written responses to prompts, and transcripts of videotaped, in-class explanations of problems. At the end of the semester, a sample of students was videotaped and their comments transcribed. All students also responded to a self-assessment generated from their own responses to the prompt "I know I understand a mathematical concept when . . ." Students also completed a midyear course evaluation.

Jen: Mini-plans for Maxi-results

The procedures I used combined our department's traditional focus on the short story genre with metacognitive activities. During the twelve-week project, we read and studied short stories in a fairly traditional manner (focusing on the literary elements of plot, conflict, setting, characterization, and theme), but at least once per week, whether in class or in small-group, we focused on some aspect of metacognition.

I had students fill out surveys about their strengths and weaknesses as writers and about their "work habits," the latter specifically focusing on planning and goal setting and revising work. Knowing that I was going to use narrative writing as my focus for the semester and as the content skill with which to use metacognitive skills, I assigned a narrative diagnostic the second week of school. Once students were finished, they assessed their own narratives using a rubric scale of one to four. I also assessed the narratives with the same rubric, but never showed the students my assessment. We spent several weeks assessing sample narratives and our own narratives. These were valuable activities because they allowed students to determine their own strengths and weaknesses, so that, when it came time to revise their original diagnostic narratives, they were able to plan what elements to add, change, delete, and so on.

During class time, my procedures involved guided practice, explicit instruction, and modeling of the metacognitive skills of planning and goal setting. I was hoping to also develop the metacognitive skills of revising, but time did not allow for this. This class time worked especially well, because students were at such different levels of skill and experience with these kinds of tasks. The group work on practice plans for imaginary and real assignments seemed to be time well spent. Students stayed on task, and worked well together. I think these activities gave all [the] students sufficient confidence that they could do these kinds of planning and goal-setting activities on their own as individuals. The final, individual project required a plan (including goals) for the project as a whole, as well as "miniplans" for several of the sections of the project. In hindsight, I should have required "miniplans" for each section, but I didn't want to overwhelm the students. However, in assessing the final products, the sections that had plans were the best ones.

The fact that I scaled back my initial goal and plan reveals one of the problems I had: the students took a long time to master each step of the planning process. I could not focus on the metacognitive skills of drafting and revising, and I felt I had to limit the amount of planning I could expect from the students. However, perhaps I was expecting too much in the beginning; perhaps, in reality, it *would* be more appropriate to focus just on planning in ninth grade, and focus on drafting and revising skills in tenth grade. Another problem was the students who left and entered in midproject. I could not use their data in my study, but I wanted the students who entered later in the semester to get the same practice with the skills, because I feel they are very important skills. Yet another problem was individual students not doing some of the work. Interestingly, though, these problems highlight the importance of qualitative research in education. There is no way to predict or control for these variables, and these kinds of problems and variables are *always* a part of education, so it's important to consider them a part of the study.

The project was about twelve weeks long, ending at Christmas break. The data I collected focused on the metacognitive skills, although I tried to also collect data on the students' narrative writing skills. This became very difficult to assess apart from the metacognitive skills, so I changed my focus to describe the changes in student use of the metacognitive skills in the context of their narrative writing. I focused on their planning and goal setting and their intentional use of narrative text conventions, as well as their ability to identify the strengths and weaknesses in their writing. I stopped collecting data once the major project was finished. I knew I could stop, because I had done both pre- and postassessments, and because I was finished with the unit itself. I had data in the form of surveys, interviews, student work, and my own observations, so I felt that I could triangulate data and ensure validity. In addition, it was Christmas vacation, and I *had* to be finished!

Data Collection

In terms of data collection, it seemed fairly obvious what methods to use, because my project focused on writing and metacognitive skills, which are somewhat more abstract, developmental skills—as opposed to a project that focused on students acquiring understanding of a single concept, such as how to solve quadratic equations. I knew my data would have to focus heavily on the students' work and responses to survey and interview questions. Observations were a bit harder to keep up with, until we got to the final project. Again, I think that perhaps because that was a more concrete activity, it changed my focus and methods of data collection. Here, I could record more specific observations of student work and attitudes to coincide with the student work itself. The only difficulty with the data collection was with the observation journal. Because the class I used for my study met in the middle of the day, I could not do any journal writing until several hours after the class had met. This made it difficult at times to recall specific things said or done in class. I don't know if there are ways to deal with this kind of problem. Perhaps jotting quick notes on Post-its to flesh out later? Perhaps choosing a class that meets at the end of the day or before a free/prep period?

Sharon: Bridging the Generations

[Before beginning the project,] I read and reread all I could find, as well as speaking to experts in the field. I sorted and synthesized this information into the various categories that emerged, for instance: program types, characteristics of successful programs, and so on. I used these categories of information to create the various components of a big plan that I felt would work for our specific program parameters (budget, time, administrative support, participants, etc). In order to create an effective program design (my definition or idea about what would constitute an effective program design evolved as I gained more information) we would need to

1. prepare the kids ahead of time for the "nursing home experience," [that is,] acclimate them to the sights, sounds, smells that they would likely encounter, and provide basic and nonthreatening information in "kid-friendly" language;
2. provide concrete-level empathy training;
3. include three components in every aspect of our design in order to optimize the positive impact of our program on attitudes. These components were:
   a. information
   b. *positive* experiences with our frail elders. Positive experiences with healthy, well elders

c. ongoing, structured opportunities for children to talk with peers
   and others about their thoughts, feelings, reactions to their intergenerational experiences.

Several components of the program design emerged due to externally im-
posed parameters, such as level of administrative support; investment of
time necessary vs. amount of time available both for planning as well as
implementation of a given lesson, visit, or project; block of time available
for research (i.e., I had only the first semester for the program implementation and ongoing data collection parts of my research project). These
program parameters created a structure which helped me in determining
such things as length of project and when to stop collecting data, designing lessons, and so on.

[While implementing my project,] I had the huge advantage of working
with an outstanding classroom teacher, Sherri, with whom I was able to
brainstorm, discuss, and rework, as needed, our program design. Through
conversation, I was able to "iron out" in advance many of the wrinkles I
would likely have had to work through had I undertaken the program entirely on my own, without anyone to bounce ideas off of. I shared with
Sherri the research, theory, and experiences of those intergenerational experts I'd read about or talked to. None of those experts, however, shared
our exact circumstances in terms of the specifics of the dynamics of our
student group, the parents with whom we were working, our administra-
tor, our schedule, our budget, and all the other variables involved.
Through conversation and planning with Sherri, I was able to make decisions ahead of time, as well as to modify plans midstream, about how to
best tailor research ideas to meet the needs of our specific students.

Data Collection

After reading articles on how others defined and measured their own intergenerational program outcomes, an attitudinal survey seemed to me to
be a logical choice for a tool to use in collecting data. I looked first for an
attitudinal survey that could be administered "pre- and post-" program implementation, as a way to gather information to answer my research question: "How can participation in an intergenerational friendly visit program
impact student attitudes toward elders and aging?" Because the question

asks "how," I needed a survey tool that would break down attitude into various indicators and observable behaviors. I found a survey that was a very good, although not perfect, match for my program, and modified it to meet our needs. For instance, I increased the font size and used a "friendlier" font that I felt would be less intimidating to fourth graders. I went "landscape" instead of "portrait" on some sheets to provide more room for children to write. I changed the questions on one section of the survey to make them specific to frail elders in a nursing home setting, rather than [referring] to elders in general. In addition to using the survey, I collected everything and anything that I thought might be useful in terms of providing ongoing feedback to genuinely guide and inform my evolving program design. Data sources included: student journal entries (both freewriting and prompted writing); unsolicited communications with parents, including parent notes containing feedback and questions and anecdotal notes from hallway and phone conversations; student feedback/questions from the class "comments and concerns" box; anecdotal notes documenting observations of student conversations with each other about the program during morning snack time, recess, and so on; photographs of student and elder interactions noting body language, eye contact, facial expression as indications of attitude; anecdotal notes in my own journal documenting student reaction to various projects, lessons, activities, discussions; products from intergenerational projects (e.g., living history books; self-portraits of elders with students; painted clay pots, etc.). We considered these products (which were not graded), in terms of quality of work, investment of time, and so on, as a reflection of attitude toward elder special friends and toward the program itself.

Lenore: Playing to Read

I began the school year with the same basic setup for centers that I had used in the past. I waited four weeks into the school year before implementing my project. This gave the students time to become familiar with the classroom routines and procedures. Once I began the project, I gradually added literacy props to the centers. I also incorporated a new thematic literacy center that changed monthly. During the implementation of my project, this center was an office, a veterinarian's clinic, a holiday cookie shop, and a pizza parlor. It took some work preparing and collecting appropriate props for the various themes, but it was well worth the extra effort. It became one of the favorite play centers in our classroom.

Many of the project methods implemented in my classroom evolved based on numerous studies and research supporting the effectiveness of literacy through play. The work of Morrow and Rand (1991), Vukelich (1993), Neuman and Roskos (1990), and Goldhaber, Lipson, Sortino and Daniels (1996–1997) was particularly helpful in developing the methodology portion of my project. Their studies demonstrated practical applications of literacy opportunities for young children within the context of developmentally appropriate practices.

I also used an environmental literacy scan (Goldhaber, Lipson, Sortino, and Daniels, 1996–1997) to assess the initial level of literacy opportunities in my classroom centers. I modified the scan to represent specific centers in my classroom. This was a useful tool to review periodically to ensure that I was maintaining and adding appropriate literacy props to the centers.

My project started at the end of September and continued through the first semester, which ended in late January. Although I stopped collecting data for the project in January, I continued with the practices that had been set up for the project throughout the remainder of the school year.

The biggest problem I had implementing my action research project was in keeping my focus on answering my research questions. So many exciting things were happening in my classroom regarding literacy that it was easy to get sidetracked and want to collect data that wouldn't necessarily help me answer my two research questions.

Data Collection

Data collection began at the very beginning of the school year. Our reading teacher administered a Concepts About Print (CAP) assessment the second week of school to my morning class of four-year-olds. The CAP assessment evaluates what students know about how print works. The CAP assessment was helpful in giving me a baseline of my students' understanding of literacy. The same assessment was given again in January. This allowed me to evaluate individual gains in understanding print. It was also an excellent indicator of the students' growth in literacy awareness as a class.

Teacher observation and anecdotal records were important components in data collection. Data were collected on an ongoing basis. I used a small tape recorder to record my observations of an activity each child engaged in during playtime. I would focus on several different students each day. Speaking into the tape recorder allowed me to keep my eyes focused on the activity as opposed to having to stop and write.

Since oral language development is such an important aspect of emergent literacy development, student dictations from art activities were also collected as data. All observations and dictations were documented and saved. Students' writing samples were collected from various centers and saved as they were made available during and after playtime.

CONCLUSION

Deciding what procedures you will follow and what data you will collect is pivotal to the success of your project. From the four teachers, you can learn some additional lessons. When you're thinking about the time frame of your study, think about the period during which you will be collecting data. As Lenore pointed out, she would be using play to teach literacy skills throughout the entire school year. But how long would she be collecting data? You need to think about what will be enough data to draw some conclusions. You won't be able to see significant changes in student achievement in a week's time. But what about in a month's time? Or will you need two months for your study? Jen's study took twelve weeks, to include the major writing project her students were doing. Lenore decided to end her study at the end of the semester. Sharon needed time to do introductory work with her students and then have enough "friendly visits" to have an impact on student attitudes toward the elderly. Let the goals of your project determine how long it should be rather than assigning an arbitrary time frame. However, you need to be realistic about how long you can collect data.

The four teachers also reveal the importance of flexibility for an action researcher. Jen's story especially shows the necessity of allowing student needs and abilities to modify your procedures. Jen began the semester with a plan, based in part on her experiences teaching previous groups of ninth graders. Her participants for the study, however, needed more time to learn the cognitive and metacognitive skills she was teaching. She had to revise her expectations and her plans.

Another lesson that the four teachers exemplify is the importance of collaboration in the action research process. The essential component of Deb's project was collaboration with the physics teacher, but the other three teachers also involved other teachers in significant ways. Jen used her department as a sounding board for what she was doing. Sharon worked with another teacher's class. This teacher also assisted Sharon in planning the "friendly visit" program, as well as in making changes as needed. The reading teacher at Lenore's school helped her collect data and provided feedback on her students' progress. Even if another teacher at your school is not directly involved in the project, you should consider consulting with one who teaches at your grade level or in your subject area when planning your procedures. Teachers can also serve as readers for your project, to check whether your findings match their experiences and to raise questions.

One of the most important lessons that can be learned from the four teachers is the importance of reflection throughout the entire process. The action researcher does not reflect only after the project to analyze and interpret the finding. She reflects constantly to note insights, to make changes, to see patterns, to recognize exceptions, and so forth. Deb had to continually check that her activities matched those of the physics teacher. Jen modified her plans to drop the unit on revision. Sharon had to make changes in her "friendly visit" program because the ones discussed in the literature didn't fit her context. Lenore watched her students closely to determine what new centers should be added and what activities were needed. While reflection occurs throughout the process, it is the heart of the next step—data analysis.

5

Findings

Now that you have completed your project, you have lots of data. One of the challenges of doing qualitative research is making sense of all the data. To make sure your study is valid, you've triangulated your data, that is, you've collected data from many sources. You've kept a journal; you probably have student work. You may have a survey or interviews, as well as other data sources. In order to answer your research question, you need to analyze these data, draw valid conclusions, and reflect on the value of your project.

DATA ANALYSIS

Data analysis involves reducing the mountains of data that you have collected into manageable chunks. You are going to reduce your data into a small set of categories. The challenge that you will face while making this reduction is making sense of large amounts of data without minimizing, distorting, oversimplifying, or misinterpreting them. Your first task then is to find those categories.

1. Review your research question. Check that this is the question for which you have been collecting data. You may have to revise your question—perhaps reword it—so that it more closely addresses the problem that you have been studying.

2. Read through all your data and look for patterns. What recurring themes do you notice?

3. When you notice a category starting to appear, code it. One easy way to do this is with colored markers. Some people cut apart the data and put them in separate files. As other categories emerge, code them also.

4. Now examine each category to see if you have enough data in it. Do you have strong evidence? Outline the evidence that you have for each category. For example, if you are looking at students' understanding of particular science concepts, you may have evidence of their ability to transfer information from one context to another. List all the pieces of evidence that suggest that transfer is occurring. You may have notes from your journal, examples of student work, tests, and so on. Do you have enough evidence to draw a conclusion? If not, you need to collect more data.

5. When you have ascertained that a category has enough data, look at it and define it. Perhaps some of your data relate to students' ability to explain what they've learned; other data refer to their ability to transfer old learning to new examples. One category might be "Explanation" and another "Transfer." Now, what do these mean in terms of students' learning? What are students able to do?

6. Look for discrepant cases. Do you have any evidence that conflicts with the majority of your data? Which students haven't achieved as well as others? In what ways? By looking at outlying evidence, you will do a more complete and much richer analysis.

One exception to this process occurs when you have predetermined your categories. One teacher wanted to know how using problem-based learning would affect her fourth graders' understanding of science concepts. In her review of literature, she came across Wiggins and McTighe's (1998) model of understanding. She decided she would structure her lessons around the ability to explain, to apply, and to think about one's own learning (i.e., metacognition). When she was ready to analyze her data, she color coded them according to these three categories.

The preceding explanation of data analysis may make the process appear more linear and simple than it actually is. The process is often recursive and complex. Categories may not be immediately evident as you read through the data, and you may have to struggle to find them. When you are reading through your data, looking for patterns, you may be gaining insights that will help you to define your categories, in addition to other insights you may have at the end of the process. After you have coded your data, you may have to read through them again, because another category emerged as you were reflecting on the significance of the data. Or you may discover that your categories don't adequately capture what you learned from your project. You may have to recode your data.

As you work through this process, you need to step back from the data. You have been intimately involved in collecting and sometimes producing the data. In order to be as objective as possible, you need some emotional distance. One way to do this is to try to become a stranger in a familiar land. Look at the data with new eyes—the eyes of a researcher and not a teacher. Question what your mind tells you is true. You have delineated your philosophy of education. Reexamine your beliefs and how they are influencing how you are seeing the data.

Simple Statistics

Even though your study is qualitative, it may be useful to quantify some of your data. For example, perhaps you want to use the results of a survey, checklist, or rubric. While you can describe the responses of open-ended questions on a survey, you can quantify the responses of objective questions if you have used a Likert scale. For example, if you have used an attitude survey, you might assign four points to "always," three points to "usually," two points to "sometimes," one point to "rarely," and zero points to "never." You could find out the mean score of students' responses to each of the questions by averaging the points.

Determining the mean, mode, and median are three ways to determine central tendencies (Mills, 2000). These three basic mathematical measures describe the distribution of values in a set of data. The *mean* is the mathematical average of all the scores. To calculate the mean, you add all the quantities in the data set and divide by the number of values you added. It should be noted that if there are a few values that are extremely high or extremely low compared with the majority of values in the data set (these values are known as "outliers"), they will distort the mean. The *median* is the middle value in the data set when the quantities are arranged numerically from smallest to largest. Half of the data points are above the median, and half are below. If there is an odd number of values in the data set, then the median is simply the middle number. If there is an even number of values in the data set, then the average of the two middle values is the median. The *mode* is the data point that appears most frequently in the data set. A data set may have more than one mode. In a data set that is evenly dispersed, known as "normally distributed," the mean, median, and mode values will be close to one another. In a data set that is not normally distributed, known as "skewed," there will be a greater difference between the mean, median, and mode values.

The mean is usually the most useful of these three statistics. Occasionally the median is the most descriptive, because the distribution of scores has outlying scores, and the mean misrepresents the data. For example, if two students were absent the day you reviewed for a test, and failed the test the next day because of their absences, the mean of the scores might not accurately describe the achievement of the class. The mode is rarely used alone because it does not show the relationship of the scores to one other.

These measures of central tendency fall under the realm of descriptive statistics. As the name implies, descriptive statistics are used to simply describe patterns evident in quantitative data. This is in contrast to interpretive statistics, which are used for purposes of comparison and prediction. In addition to measures of central tendency, one measure of variation, the *range*, may also provide useful information about the values in a data set and what they represent. The range is the difference between the highest value and the lowest value in the data set.

To exemplify these terms, let's look at a set of scores that a group of sophomore geometry students received on an algebra skills inventory. There were forty-five questions on the inventory. Scores represent the number of questions students answered correctly. Twenty-nine students took the inventory. Table 5.1 shows the scores.

From this table, you can see that the mean score is 37.24. Some calculation is required to determine the mean. Add all 29 of the scores together. The total is 1,080. Divide that number by 29 (the number of

Table 5.1. Scores

25
27
31
31
32
34
34
35
36
37
37
37
38
38
38
39
39
39
39
40
40
40
41
41
41
42
43
43
43

Total	1080
Mean	37.24

scores in this data set). That value—37.24—is the mean. In other words, the average score for students in this class on this 45-question inventory is 37.24.

From table 5.1 you can also note that the range of scores is from 25 to 43. Table 5.2 indicates the range.

Table 5.2. Range

	Number	Minimum	Maximum	Mean
Skill Scores	29	25	43	37.24

There is another useful way to display the scores, a *frequency distribution* table. Scores are arranged from lowest to highest. The numbers in the "frequency" column represent the number of students who achieved a particular score, or the "frequency" with which a score was earned. For example, 1 student out of the 29 scored a 25; 2 students scored a 31. The number in the "percent" column represents the percent of the 29 students who earned a particular score. For example, 3.4 percent of the students (1 out of 29) scored a 25, while 6.9 percent of the students (2 out of 29) scored a 31. Table 5.3 shows a frequency distribution using the scores in table 5.1.

When scores are organized in a frequency distribution table, several measures of the central tendency and variation of the data become apparent. First, the range of values is obvious. In this example, the low score is 25 and the high score is 43, so the range of the values is 18, or 43 minus 25.

Another measure that is evident in a frequency distribution table is the mode. The mode is the most frequently occurring value or values in the data. In this data set, the score of 39 is the mode because more students (4) achieved that score than any of the others.

Because this data set has an odd number of values (29), the median is the one middle score, or the 15th score in the table. The frequency values are totaled to determine which score is the 15th score in the table. The

Table 5.3.   **Frequency Distribution**

Scores	Frequency	Percent
25	1	3.4
27	1	3.4
31	2	6.9
32	1	3.4
34	2	6.9
35	1	3.4
36	1	3.4
37	3	10.3
38	3	10.3
39	4	13.8
40	3	10.3
41	3	10.3
42	1	3.4
43	3	10.3
Total	29	100.0

number 38 is this middle score. There are 14 scores below 38 in the table and 14 scores above 38 in the table. Table 5.4 is a variation of the first frequency distribution (table 5.3) that allows you to determine the mean as well as the frequency.

You can organize and display data in a variety of different ways. One way is with a table or chart like the frequency distribution tables 5.3 and 5.4. A second, somewhat more visual way to display data is with a bar graph. In figure 5.1, using the algebra skills inventory data, the range (25–43) and the mode (39) can be clearly seen.

Table 5.4. **Frequency Distribution and Mean**

Scores	Frequency	Percent
25	1	3.4
27	1	3.4
31	2	6.9
31		
32	1	3.4
34	2	6.9
34		
35	1	3.4
36	1	3.4
37	3	10.3
37		
37		
38	3	10.3
38		
38		
39	4	13.8
39		
39		
39		
40	3	10.3
40		
40		
41	3	10.3
41		
41		
42	1	3.4
43	3	10.3
43		
43		
1080	29	100.0

Mean
37.24

Algebra Skills Inventory

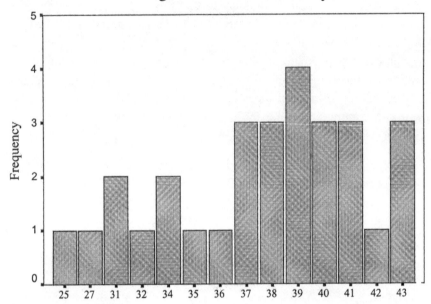

Figure 5.1.   Bar Graph

The pie chart offers another visual way of displaying the same data. A pie chart can be used only if you have percentages that add up to 100 percent. In other words, the pie represents 100 percent of the scores. Each "piece" shows the percent of students receiving a certain score. In the last column of table 5.4, the percentage of students receiving each score is noted. This value was calculated by dividing the frequency value by the total number of scores. These percentages can be displayed by dividing a circle or "pie" into sectors or "slices." The relative size of each wedge corresponds to the percentage in the last column of the frequency distribution table. Figure 5.2 is an example of a pie chart. Because of the many "slices," this chart is difficult to read.

Consistency

If you are averaging scores on a test, you have a fairly objective measure of student learning. But what if you are assessing student work that is more subjective? What if you are evaluating student writing and using a

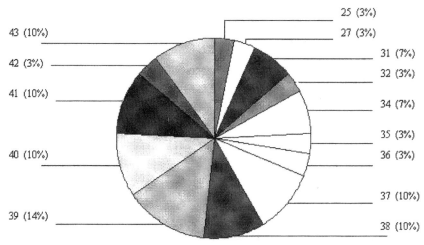

Figure 5.2. Algebra Skills Inventory

rubric to determine a score? Will you score the paper the same way that someone else will? Will you give the art project the same grade as another assessor? To diminish subjectivity, you can use two or more readers/assessors to look at student work.

You need to choose your readers/assessors carefully. They need to be looking at the student work through the same lens as you. Make sure they share your understanding of the assignment and the assessment tool, and have the same concept of quality that you do. They will need some training to ensure that they are assessing properly. Give the assessors some examples of excellent, good, average, and poor work as benchmarks. Discuss why these samples represent varying degrees of quality. Then practice assessing a few samples together.

After the assessors have completed their task, you need to check to see whether their scores are close to each other. In other words, you need to check for reliability. If the scores are the same, you have some assurance that the scores reflect the quality of the work. If the scores are different, the assessors can discuss the scores and try to reach consensus, or a third reader can determine the score. In any case, the assessors must be trained to use the assessment tool so that they have the same understanding as you of the qualities that are being assessed. With practice and feedback, the assessors should become relatively consistent in their use of the assessment tool.

DATA INTERPRETATION

Your project has been leading to this point—what does it all mean? You've asked a question, you've collected data, you've organized your data into categories, and now you're ready to answer the question.

When you are interpreting the data, remember that you need to *synthesize* them. You are not interpreting your journal entries and then student work and then the survey results. You need to interpret your categories and use the various data sources as evidence. You are interpreting how students have learned (e.g., how they have been able to explain certain math concepts) by examining what you have recorded in your journal or what you have noticed on the videotapes, what you have assessed in student work, or what you have discovered in the student surveys.

Consider a few things before you start your interpretation.

It's just as important to explore why students haven't learned something as it is to investigate how they have. Imagine what would happen if drug manufacturers "proved" that every drug worked so that they could sell it. It's important to know which drugs don't work for certain diseases. Likewise, if students didn't meet your objectives, it's important to recognize and understand that.

Therefore, be as objective as you can be in interpreting the results. As we discussed with regard to data analysis, you need to have enough evidence to make claims, and you need to look at the evidence with new eyes. You need to make the familiar strange. Look for discrepant cases. You have been the teacher-researcher, so there will be a certain amount of bias. Recognize your subjectivity by examining your assumptions about teaching and learning. Describe any impact that your subjectivity may have had on your study.

Don't generalize the results to all students. Even though you may not explicitly state a generalization, beware of implying it. If you conclude that "service learning develops empathy and caring in children," you are implying that it does so for all children. What you have found applies only to your classroom. Be careful you don't make claims that you can't substantiate. Whatever you did in your classroom may have been successful with that group of students, but perhaps it won't be with another group. Or perhaps it will. From your study you cannot predict what will happen with another group of students. This lack of generalizability does not diminish the importance of your study. Your study is informative for other teachers, who will be able to determine for themselves its applicability. If you share your findings with them, you are adding to the body of knowledge regarding teaching and learning.

Don't claim causality. Don't say *x* caused *y*. Just indicate what happened. You did *x* and *y* happened. Did *x* cause *y* to happen or was it some other variable? You don't know for sure. Your best guess is that *x* was the cause, but you can't know for certain.

Be careful with your language. Use words like "seem" and "suggest" rather than "prove" or "cause." For example, write "The data suggest that students' ability to think about their own learning improved through the use of reflective writing," rather than "The use of reflective writing caused students' ability to think about their own learning to improve."

It's a good idea, when you have completed your data interpretation, to have someone who is familiar with your project read it to verify its accuracy. If your students are old enough, you could ask two or three of them to read your study. If you have paraprofessionals or parents who have been assisting in your classroom while you have implemented your project, they could serve as readers. Perhaps another teacher who teaches your subject or grade level could help you to consider the trustworthiness of your findings.

Significance and Value of the Findings

After you have analyzed your data and interpreted the results, you have one remaining task. You need to draw conclusions and discuss the significance of the findings. You need to draw meaning from the results. In other words, you need to ask the question "So what?" Why is what you have found valuable for you as a teacher, for your students as learners, for other teachers as lifelong learners? What implications does your project have beyond the limited time of your study? These questions will push your thinking to greater depths about the meaning of your project.

Trustworthiness

Before you prepare your final report, you need to do a few more checks for validity. Here are some questions to help you further evaluate the validity of your study.

Trustworthiness of the Data

Do you have enough data? It's better to have too many data than too few.

1. Have you collected any incidences of data that disprove your findings? Are there any students who haven't performed as you might have hoped?
2. Are your students being honest? In interviews, for example, students might be trying to please you with their answers. Report any possibilities that this kind of dishonesty might exist.
3. Have any significant events affected your students during the course of your study that might have affected the results? For example, was there a fire at the school?
4. Have you selected a representative group of students?
5. Have any of the students left your class during the course of the study?
6. Do your students know that they are part of a study? Is this influencing their behavior?
7. Do you have any other observers in your classroom? Is their presence influencing student behavior?

Trustworthiness of the Researcher

1. Are you overly subjective? Have you been as objective as possible?
2. Have you checked your assumptions and beliefs?

Trustworthiness of the Inferences

1. Are you oversimplifying what you have found?
2. Could changes in achievement be attributed to developmental changes in the children rather than to your activities with them?
3. Are you drawing conclusions that the data don't support?
4. Have you considered all possible explanations?
5. Are you overgeneralizing?
6. Have you checked your findings with other teachers, parents, or students?
7. Have you found other studies that have shown similar results?

Reexamine your conclusions in light of these questions. Qualify any statements you make about your findings if necessary. Revise your findings so that they honestly, accurately, and clearly reflect the reality of your project.

QUALITY OF THE REPORTING

Once you are ready to write up the findings, you need to consider the quality of your reporting. You want to apply the same standards of academic rigor that guided your research. One consideration of quality is reliability. "Reliability" refers to the degree to which the inferences in the findings are consistent across time. Could another researcher do your study and get the same results? Quantitative studies often are replicated. Qualitative studies cannot be replicated in the same sense. The context of the investigation will always be different. But what if another teacher wanted to implement your methodology with her students? Have you described your study in enough detail to allow her to do a similar study?

The concern with reliability can be addressed by writing thick, rich description of what you did and what you found. Let your reader see and hear what occurred in your classroom. Describe your students and what they did and said. You may be reporting in a narrative. What happened first, next, later? This elaboration will increase the reliability of your study. Describe what happened with most of your students; however, also describe any discrepant cases. Were there any students who did not react like the other students in the study? The reader will be able to tell whether or not your study can be translated to her classroom.

TEACHER VOICES

The four teachers will now explain how they analyzed their data. They will focus on how they read through their data, looking for patterns. Two of the teachers had preexisting categories. Deb's categories came from the work of Wiggins and McTighe on understanding, and Sharon's came from the survey that she revised. Jen and Lenore's categories emerged from their data. All the teachers used some sort of coding system. After their data were reduced to smaller categories, they analyzed and interpreted the findings. In the next chapter, they will talk more about this process.

Deb: Searching for Understanding

When I began the project, I had what I would call a very naïve definition of "understanding." If a student knew why he or she was performing a certain mathematical manipulation in order to solve a problem, I thought the student was demonstrating understanding. As part of my research, I came across the work done by Grant Wiggins, and I, in fact, heard him speak. Wiggins presented a framework for understanding that involved a variety of facets. Since this project was completed, Wiggins slightly revised his framework to include six areas that indicate understanding. Wiggins's categories at the time included sophistication of insight, perspective, and know-how.

Wiggins's model was very explicit about what understanding in each of the categories included. I had videotapes transcribed, and I had copies of all student work from the unit and semester course evaluations, and I had my own journal entries. I read through all the data and coded references to "behaviors" described in each of Wiggins's categories. I used different colored highlighters to do the coding. I reported my findings category by category.

Jen: Looking at Metacognition

This part was the most difficult only because of the previously mentioned problems with trying to analyze narrative writing skills apart from the metacognitive skills. When I finally decided to keep them together, I could proceed more quickly. I highlighted data in four different colors to correspond with my categories of data: strengths and weaknesses, planning, goal setting, intentional use of text conventions. Then I used corresponding colors of index cards to synthesize the info and to write down ideas and information I wanted to include in each section of my data analysis. I looked for students to use as case studies, but there was such a wide range of results, that it became impossible to choose three or four students who could accurately represent the whole class. I finally decided to describe the work and responses of several students at various levels in each category, so that the reader could get a better picture of the range of student work.

Sharon: Examining Attitudes about the Elderly

I used a percent value to compare responses on the pre and post attitudinal survey. I then looked for patterns in "pre- and post-" results and considered what these results might suggest. I used the categories and questions on the modified attitudinal survey as a framework for sorting and analyzing data from all of my other sources. I considered, for each question/category of information, whether or not this other data (journals, anecdotal notes, etc.) seemed to support the results and implications of the survey data. I used lots of highlight markers and color-coded file folders to allow me to visually sort and organize piles and piles and piles of information. The back room of my house was off limits to everyone except me for about nine months. Suggestions I would have for others about how to analyze data without losing sanity: Have a plan in place based on research you've read and what seems logical; have lots of room where you can leave your work spread out over time; invest in color-coded files, highlighters, Post-its, and vertical plastic file–type organizers; be flexible in adjusting your data analysis methods. More reasonable procedures/frameworks may become apparent once you dive in.

Lenore: Exploring Literacy Behaviors

Once the data were collected, I prioritized and categorized the information. I looked at examples of independent literacy behaviors, peer interactive literacy behaviors, and teacher/student interactive literacy behaviors. I wanted to see what types of literacy behaviors were exhibited. I also looked for patterns in the data to see if certain centers were used more frequently than others were. Finally, I looked for a connection between teacher modeling of literacy behaviors and student awareness and use of literacy behaviors.

The results of the CAP assessments from September and January provided concrete measurable results, making them easy to analyze. I should note the CAP assessment is usually administered to five-year-old kindergarten students at the end of their senior kindergarten year rather than to four-year-old junior kindergarten students at the beginning of the year. I was especially pleased to have the reading teacher report that the students seemed enthusiastic and excited about literacy when she did the January assessment. She noted that a child's attitude toward literacy is a key factor in literacy development. The reading teacher's observations reassured me that I was on the right track with my project.

CONCLUSION

As Jen pointed out, analyzing your data can be a difficult process. Sharon gives practical advice about keeping your sanity as you sift through piles of data: If at all possible, find a space that you can use to keep all your data. Try color-coding your data if you are a visual learner. (There are computer programs that will sort your data for you, but you have to input them.)

Having preexisting categories that come from a theoretical framework will simplify the process. However, you still need to be open to other categories that might emerge from your data. In the next chapter, the teachers will go into more detail about their data analysis and interpretation as they continue to discuss how they ensured validity in their action research projects.

6

Validity Revisited

The last two chapters will revisit validity and value in action research by calling on the four teachers whose stories have been shared throughout this book. Some books on action research discuss validity only in terms of data collection, that is, collecting sufficient and diverse kinds of data for triangulation. This book has emphasized the necessity of thinking about and using strategies to ensure validity throughout the entire process. The four teachers reinforce this position in the following conversation.

Looking to practicing action researchers to define validity is supported by Zeichner and Noffke (2001) in their extensive analysis of the issues surrounding practitioner research, a broader category into which action research fits. They have raised the question of who sets the criteria for trustworthiness—that is, validity—and quality in this kind of research. They conclude, "In our view, those educators [who conduct the research] must have a say in how the issues get resolved with regard to their own work and in practitioner research generally" (p. 323).

So we turn to Deb, Sharon, Jen, and Lenore, who gathered together to share their views on what gave their projects validity. As you are reading their dialogue, note some of the common themes that emerge from their discussion.

1. Maintaining the *soundness of subject matter*
2. *Collaborating* with peers
3. *Revisiting the theory* in the literature review throughout the process

4. *Revisiting the research question* throughout the process
5. *Triangulating data*
6. *Remaining objective*, constantly asking, "What am I seeing?"
7. *Accepting the messiness of data analysis*, spending time with the data, and being patient
8. *Not claiming causality or overgeneralizing*
9. Looking for and analyzing *discrepant cases*

Here is their conversation with my commentary.

EILEEN: The first question that I'd like to ask is, how did you think about validity while you were doing your projects?

DEB: The first time I was really conscious of thinking of that I guess was when I was designing my procedures. Because I wanted to make sure that what I was doing was mathematically sound because I was trying to integrate calculus and physics together. And in that process, I was resequencing the calculus concepts. So the textbook I was using had them in a different place than the way I was going to present them. So I wanted something that would kind of verify that what I was doing made sense mathematically. *[Soundness of content: You should not do anything that isn't pedagogically sound for the sake of the study. Note that teachers use their own language to talk about validity. Here Deb is using "verify."]* So I drew on other members of the department at the time. And what I asked them to read wasn't really student work at that point, but it was my procedures. "Here's what I'm thinking about doing. Does this make sense to you?" So I was conscious of it then, and I was thinking of it in terms of validity of procedure at that point, to make sure that I wasn't violating something mathematically by doing that. *[Collaboration: Deb used her colleagues to ensure that her procedures would lead to valid findings.]*

SHARON: I would say the same thing for my intergenerational project. When I was doing my review of the literature, I had a really hard time narrowing things down. But one of the things that kept popping up over and over was human developmental theory. So I had this sort of gut feeling about what I was researching and what needed to happen and what do these kids need and what do these elders need. And then I was able to look at the human developmental theory and all these different pieces of literature, and that sort of verified for me that I wasn't just sort of pulling this from the sky, that there really was something valid—if that's the right way to use the word—in what I was looking for. So I had that as kind of a focus point for part of my structure for how I was putting things together. *[Theory: Sharon used human developmental theory as a framework for her study. Because her study was theory-driven she had more confidence that her study would have validity.]*

JEN: What I remember being really helpful was that summer when we were starting our project . . . [asking,] is this a good question? When I started, my question was, how would teaching metacognitive skills affect kids' narrative writing skills? And then I remember the light bulb going on and saying, well, I can't answer that because there are too many other things that will affect their narrative writing skills. So that made me make my question much more specific so that it could be valid. *[Revisiting the question: Jen revised her question to increase the possibility that she would have valid results.]*

And I had to try to find connections between metacognition and narrative writing. So it was a combination of looking at the literature to get a research base and talking to colleagues to check with the English department about the narrative piece. *[Theory and collaboration: Like Deb, Jen talked to her department about her project, as well as consulting theorists and researchers in the two fields.]*

LENORE: And talking to colleagues helped me too. Our reading teacher was very instrumental in helping when I started implementing literacy through play. She gave an assessment in September and again in January. The things that she noticed when she was in the classroom really helped me to process and reinforce what I was doing and say, okay, I'm on track with what I'm doing, it makes sense. *[Collaboration: Lenore found working with the reading teacher at her school to be very useful.]*

DEB: You talked about the review of literature. And when I got to the part of analyzing the data, I was still working under a real, I think, naïve concept of understanding. Because that was part of my question, how would this connection, or how could it or would it, promote student understanding. And to me initially, understanding was just, can they explain why they're doing what they're doing instead of just going through mathematical manipulation. But it was through the things that I got from the review of literature that gave me a framework for understanding, that I had something to hook these things into then. And that was really important for me in terms of saying, oh, okay, yeah, they do understand because I can now show in three ways how that understanding is expressed. *[Theory: Deb found a theoretical framework in the literature that helped her see understanding in a more sophisticated way. This framework helped her to collect and analyze data.]*

JEN: So that would seem to me to make your results more valid, because the results are specific to that definition of understanding.

DEB: But that wasn't something I went into the process with, that understanding of understanding, you know. It grew as I did the research. And the other thing you mentioned, Jen, about the questions. But it became, as you said, very clear as you started looking at them that I would have no way of knowing what the answers to some of those questions were. And then one by one, they sort of fell out, and I was left with the most important thing. *[Questions: Like Jen, Deb kept revising her questions to make sure they could be answered validly.]*

SHARON: I mentioned before about human developmental theory and what I picked up from the literature there. And after I got done reading about those kinds of things, I was able then to read about programming models. And those made sense to me then, and I was able, because of what I had read about human development theory, I was able to read about the programming models in different pieces of research and understand what they were saying as far as, is this a well-developed program or not. So that in order for me to know if what I saw was accurate, it has to do with the kind of program that I put together. And because it's a really new field, I talked to people who are current practitioners with this stuff. And they told me, okay, you know what, your results are not going to be valid unless you give these kids opportunities for interaction with healthy, well elders also, because otherwise, you might actually be contributing to negative stereotypes. So had I not had that piece of information, then my results would have been quite different, I'm sure.

So the way that my program was put together has everything to do with whether or not my results are valid. And I checked and I double-checked and I looked at the literature and I talked to people. And I feel very confident that what I reported was valid. *[Theory and collaboration: Sharon used the advice of experts and the information she found in her review of literature to design a program that could lead to valid results. She realized she needed to expose her students to well elders as well as frail ones. She learned that if she had only taken children to a nursing home to visit frail elders, her data would have been skewed. These experiences may have negatively affected the children's attitudes toward elders.]*

EILEEN: When you were collecting your data, I'm sure you were concerned about having enough data so that you could draw accurate conclusions. So could you talk a little bit about how you collected your data?

SHARON: I can say that I started off OK knowing what I wanted—I was looking at attitudes and beliefs, and golly, how do we, you know, you can't crawl inside someone's head. So we decided—and again, after looking at all of the literature on it—what would be the best way to do this. And I found a presurvey that—a survey that could be used as a preassessment and a postassessment. So we took that, and I looked at how the authors of that survey used it and how they analyzed data with it. And it was for a different group. It was written for children who are much older, and the study was set up differently. So I took it and changed it so that it would fit what we were doing and would measure—I put it in kid-friendly language and all that, again, because we wanted to be valid. And again, I ran it by lots of people, because the more sets of eyes that look at that, the better. And so that's what I started with. *[Theory: Sharon wanted to use a preexisting survey that had validity. By changing the survey, she may have affected its validity in terms of traditional research. However, in her action research project, the minimal, careful changes gave her survey results credibility.]*

And we also had a plan—and I say "we," because I was lucky enough to work with a classroom teacher on this, because I don't have my own classroom, so that was a big, huge benefit right from the get-go, bouncing ideas off of people. But I used that survey as a starting point. And I knew that that was something, while this isn't per se quantifiable research, it was something that I could get a percent on, the way kids scored in different arenas. And then from that, well, okay. So that was one piece. And then also, we looked at student journals, because that was a hardcopy of something that we would have. We gave parent surveys which we created ourselves, again running it by lots of people and again looking back on— always looking at the literature, what's out there already, what kind of results, and literature that shows both successful and not successful kinds of things. What worked, what didn't, why, all of that. So we created those. *[Triangulation: Note that Sharon also created her own survey to give to parents. You won't always be able to find a survey that you can modify.]* And then what I did all along the way is, every time we did something—and again, everything we did was very well thought out. Because we had limited—like everybody—limited time, lots we wanted to accomplish. We wanted to integrate as much as we could and all those sorts of things. But every time we would do anything, I would think, oh, I could use this as data. I could use this as data. *[Triangulation and collaboration: Sharon collected many different kinds of data and used her partner teacher to help her during this process.]*

For instance, one of the activities that we did, we had the art teacher work with us. And there was some—I forget exactly what it was now, but at Kohl's here in town, it was Senior Awareness Day or something. And so at the nursing home, one of the projects that we did is, we had the students work with their elder special friends to draw self-portraits of the child, usually it was two children paired up with a resident. So it would be the two children and the resident. They were to draw a self-portrait of the three of them, working as a team, on grocery bags. And then give those out to people. I mean, I didn't come up with that project. So anyway, what we noticed when we looked at all of the work that they did, the seniors were almost always in the middle. They were almost always much bigger. They were—they had much more detail than the kids. So I took it to the art specialist and I said, help me evaluate this. What does this mean? And we got out some books, and she said, well, it looks like the most important person here is the senior. And I go, oh, this is data. And I mean that's kind of what we did all along. How can we use this to support what it is we think we're seeing? Or conversely, if this doesn't, if this is a piece of—I don't know if "evidence" is the right word—but evidence that says, oh, wait a minute, put the brakes on. Maybe what you think you're seeing isn't really what you are seeing. It helped to keep us objective, because, of course, we know what we want to see. *[Collaboration and objectivity: Sharon used expert advice when she noticed something in the data that she was unsure of. She constantly questioned what she was seeing to check to make sure she was remaining objective.]*

JEN: I did surveys in the beginning to see where kids were at the beginning [of the semester in terms of planning skills], which was nowhere. But that's good [to know where to begin my instruction], you know. Otherwise, I've got to start over. And I used student journals too. And sometimes it was specific questions about their skills. So it was journals and it was my own journal of observations and just tons of student work. Because what I was evaluating was their writing. And it was different kinds of writing. Sometimes it was writing down their plan for how to do their assignment. And we did a lot of practice, starting with really small, you know, if you have to write an essay about this, how are you going to go about planning to do that. And then at the end, it became planning for a big project. So it was all these little pieces of data on smaller assignments building up to the big ones, where they had practice for that. *[Triangulation: Jen used multiple data sources to get lots of information on her students' learning before she drew any firm conclusions.]*

SHARON: When you say you would interview them or evaluate their writing, I'm curious to know, did you use like some kind of a rubric, or how did you evaluate that to try to keep it objective?

JEN: Because we were doing narrative writing, we had a rubric that all of the freshman English teachers were using, so they [the freshmen] did an initial essay. And then we went through with the rubric and they graded their own story. And they were very accurate. Because then I went through and graded them. Then we looked at other stories that people had written and then looked at short stories and we talked about and used the rubric all the way through. So that was helpful for them. *[Triangulation and objectivity: The rubric was a useful data collection tool because Jen could compare her students' perceptions about their writing with hers.]*

And that was what was hard, because I was collecting data on their narrative writing and their metacognition skills at the same time. And I kept trying to separate them and I couldn't. Finally, I just said, I can't, I don't know how to separate them. And then finally Eileen said, well, then don't. I had to do them both at the same time, which makes sense, because when you're writing, you're doing those skills all the time anyway. So once I accepted the fact that I had to just collect it all at the same time and deal with analyzing it later, then I got a lot more done, because I just kept taking stuff in and kept talking to the kids and just writing more stuff down. *[Messiness of data: When you're collecting data, don't worry about the categories. They may begin to emerge as you are doing your study, but you don't need to categorize the data as you are collecting it. You will have lots of data that will be assigned to categories during the analysis and interpretation phases.]*

DEB: When I began the project, I asked the kids to tell me how they knew when they understood a mathematical concept. How did they know that they understood it? And I got a variety of different things. "I can explain it to other people," "I can work independently," a number of those. And I collated those and there were definite categories just in their responses. And then that became the self-assessment rubric that I asked them to fill out halfway through the semester: "How are you doing?" "How do you feel you're doing on these things?" And they rated themselves and I rated them, without looking at their ratings. And we were very close. There was some discrepancy. But for the most part, I rated them very similarly to how they rated themselves. And that's a nice thing with older kids, that they can give you that kind of feedback. *[Messiness of data: In Deb's case, categories began to emerge during the study from students' reports of their metacognition. Because Deb recognized those categories, she developed another data collection tool, the self-assessment rubric.]*

EILEEN: Lenore, you have kindergartners. Tell us about how you collected your data.

LENORE: We did a "concepts about print" assessment the second week of school, which is an assessment usually given at the end of senior kindergarten. It assesses what children understand about print. Do they know where the front cover of the book is? Do they know where the back is? Do they know that you read from left to right? Do they know the letters of the alphabet? Can they show you a word? Can they show you a letter? It looks at basic concepts about print. We did the assessment in September and at the end of January. The growth was phenomenal in what they gained over those few months. That was wonderful data to have. *[Triangulation: Like Lenore, you may be able to use some assessment tool that your school or district already uses.]*

I did a lot of teacher observation. All of a sudden, I'm looking for things that I didn't know I was necessarily looking for. It was eye-opening to me to go, wow, they're really doing this. Then I started to question, were they doing that before and I just didn't see it? There were more literacy props and things in the classroom, so I know that they were using more tools than they were using before, but they might have been exhibiting some of those literacy behaviors before. That was something I struggled with throughout the project. *[Remaining objective: Teacher observation is an important data collection method. However, Lenore had to constantly question herself to check that she was seeing what was there and not what she wanted to be there.]*

I collected a lot of writing samples whenever they would write. At the end of the day, I would go back through the living center and the block and find all sorts of fun things they had written. It was just a lot of collecting and a lot of watching.

DEB: And I would think that would be especially true, the watching part, with little kids because you can't ask them to write a story. They can't do that.

LENORE: Lots of watching. I used a little tape recorder, because I didn't want to stop and look down and write because I would miss what they were doing. So I just kept a little tape recorder and I would just talk into that. *[Triangulation: Keeping a journal is an invaluable data collection tool because it provides a daily log of observations and reflections. Lenore found that taping her comments was more convenient and more immediate than writing them down.]*

EILEEN: So you have all this data. Could you talk about the process that you went through to analyze the data, to make sure that you would get valid results? It sounds easy to say, oh, well, just read through your data, look for patterns. But the process is really messy and difficult. So could you talk a little bit about what you were thinking when you were analyzing your data?

SHARON: For me, it was very painstaking, because it involved making a lot of choices. And I'm sometimes not good at choices. And I think that for anybody, when you're feeling overwhelmed, you sort of downshift a little bit. And it's just like, oh, okay, somebody help me here. So what I did is, I did it in stages, in steps. And I did have a big area, so I could spread my things out. Because we had artwork, we had my journal, we had the kids' journals, we had all these parent notes on different sizes of paper, tons of stuff just everywhere. And what I ended up doing was getting a bunch of highlighters in different colors, and I looked through—and again, I had Sherrie, the teacher that I was working with, help me with this. And so we could go back and forth about, okay, what are we seeing here and what might this indicate, what might this mean. *[Messiness of data and objectivity: When you're done collecting data, you will be overwhelmed with the amount of material you have. Data analysis and interpretation require patience, organization, and reflection. Sharon had the added benefit of having a critical friend help her sort through the data and draw objective conclusions.]*

And we tried to be really careful about not saying cause and effect or here, this proves this. But rather, here's what we're seeing, here's what we think this might mean, maybe, [what] this suggests. For instance, again back to the grocery paper bags, here's what we're seeing. Wow. All of these have the senior person's pictures bigger and/or in the center and/or with more detail, more color, more carefully done. What might this suggest? This is a pattern that we're seeing. *[Not claiming causality: Sharon was careful to describe what she found but to not assert what caused it. Sharon felt that her intergenerational program had caused these changes in her students' attitudes, but she recognized that she could never be sure. Her research design was such that it could not show causality.]*

EILEEN: Like empathy?

SHARON: Yes, like empathy. I remember one of the questions was "Do you think someone in a nursing home could learn something from you?" and "Do you think you could learn something from someone in a nursing home?" And we sort of put them together with a more general heading. And again, when we did that, when we looked at analyzing, we did look back at the literature and what did we pull out so that we knew that the way we were grouping those questions and those responses made sense according—we weren't just saying, I think number 2 will go over here because it looks like a question that would look good with red on it, and the pink would be—I mean, there was a rhyme and reason, definitely, to the way we categorized things. So we used the survey as sort of our framework. And we had our yellow questions and our pink questions—I'm very visual—and our blue questions. And for some of the things, I actually photocopied because I didn't want to destroy my original data. So I would make photocopies, which, I mean I had a lot of stuff, lot of stuff, and I'd color-code and I'd put on piles and cut up and put—this question goes here, this question goes here. And the whole time, of course, thinking, you know, sometimes I need to work smart, because if I don't, I'm going to be here for five years and the world will be a different place.

So we did that. And then we took all [the rest of the data]. For instance, I've got all my categories now based on my survey, from my survey and in different categories. Now let's look at the unsolicited parent responses. Where does this one fall, what category? It goes over in the category A or category B or category C. The same thing, then, with the student journals. And there too, we made photocopies of things. We'd highlight, we'd cut up, put this over here. Then once we had all of our data separated, now we have to look at, okay, what is it telling us. Is it telling us, yes, that, gosh, there's been a growth in empathy, or no, there hasn't been growth in empathy. Or, yes, these kids have generalized empathy not only to elders but to children who are different in any way, you know, racially or learning styles or whatever. So we had to really sit down and look at all of that. And there were times, again, sometimes it was real obvious. But again, there were times when we really had to look back. It was a very slow process. Look back at the research and what does it say. That was really how I analyzed that data. And then looking at the "pre- and the post-"— I guess one more thing, looking at the "pre- and post-" responses to those questions, what percentage, in what way were the responses different, and was it an increase or a decrease in a certain type response? What might this suggest? And then, does my other data support that, or does it not support that? And then, if it did, why? And have a little discussion about that. And if it didn't, why? And have a little discussion about that. *[Theory and triangulation: By going back to the survey Sharon found in her literature review, Sharon found categories for analyzing her data. She used other sources to corroborate what she learned from the survey.]*

So I think that that piece of looking at why or why not adds to the validity. Because what we're saying is—gosh, this is hard to put into words—what we're saying is, we're not just going to make this a contrived thing. This is what I want to see, and, therefore, this is how I'm seeing it. We're really like, wait a minute, this doesn't make sense. The survey says this, but this parent letter says this. Now why might that be? And then looking back over everything and again, saying not definitely, this, this and this. But, you know, that this might suggest that, or here's a possible reason for this discrepancy. *[Triangulation, objectivity, and discrepant cases: By checking to see if she found the same thing in multiple data sources, Sharon was able to assure herself that she was being objective and finding results that had actually occurred. Her use of discrepant cases further ensured validity. By looking at students who did not follow the same pattern as other students, Sharon developed a richer understanding of what happened during her project.]*

So I think that the data analysis—I guess all the way through this whole thing, I mean, I was really careful about paying attention to validity. Because, you know what, I worked really hard on this, and I want people to believe me. I want people to believe that what I'm saying is really, really what I saw, you know.

JEN: And I did a similar thing [in struggling to make sense of my data], because I was trying to do two things as one, which someone said to me—I think it might have been you, Deb—whatever you pick [for your study], pick something that's really concrete and really easy to measure. And I picked writing [which isn't easy to measure]. Okay. But I remember sitting in Eileen's office and saying, I have all this data and I know that part of what I want to—the reason I'm doing all this with my kids—[is] because I want their skills to be better and I want their writing skills to be better, specifically narrative writing, where they put in plot and character and theme, setting. But also, that they were using these particular text conventions to get there, you know, like figures of speech and imagery and all that kind of stuff.

So what was helpful then was to go back to my review of the literature. And what was I researching? Duh, you know. Okay, well, here, planning skills. Oh, here, I have all this data about planning skills. So I did the highlighter colors too, because I had actually done—and I'm not that visual—but I had done my note cards, like when I was researching, I had done those in colored note cards. So then I just matched the colors in my data. So I was like, here's stuff about planning, which is all on my purple cards, so it gets purple. So that's finally when I figured out and sat down with Eileen, and we kind of laid out, okay, do these four things [i.e., categories]. Because this is what your data is on anyway. And these are more concrete things that are easier to talk about and easier to say, here's where they were in the beginning, here's where they were at the end.

So I kept still going back to my research. When I started to get bogged down, I started to go, I have too much stuff here. If I just kept focusing on that, I go, okay, I don't need this yet. I can come back to this later. And it forced me to sort of compartmentalize things a little bit, just so it was more manageable because there was just so much stuff. *[Theory and messiness of data: Instead of choosing something that was easy to describe and/or measure, Jen chose a topic about which she felt passionate. Jen was able to describe how her students' planning and writing changed over time by going back to the literature review to see how her data aligned with what other research had shown. By using theory found in the literature and examining and reexamining the data, Jen discovered categories that were useful in capturing her students' achievements.]*

SHARON: You need some structure. *[Messiness of data: Notice how data management became easier for all the teachers once a structure was determined.]*

JEN: Yeah. So that was helpful just to keep going back to my research and keep focusing on what's the reason I'm doing this anyway, what do I want the kids to do, what is my hope that by the end they'll get to do. Knowing that they won't all necessarily get there, but what is my purpose in doing this. I had to keep going back to that question. And then that would help me refocus on my data and put it into categories. That was helpful. *[Revisit the question: When you are immersed in all your data, it's easy to lose track of your question. By revisiting your question, you will be able to tighten your focus and eliminate irrelevant data.]*

LENORE: I did the same thing with the color coding, saying, okay, this goes here, and putting them all into categories and seeing where they all fit in. The depth of play, I know, was one category that actually surprised me. That wasn't something that I thought about when I was doing that project.

EILEEN: How did you find that category?

LENORE: One of the thematic centers we had was an office. We talked about offices and the children knew that their parents went to offices. Then we went down to the school office and the secretary showed us her office. We went back to our classroom, and I turned them loose on our new center. We had lots of fun things in there for them to play with. For the first two weeks, there was a lot of parallel play. They didn't really interact with each other. They seemed to have fun playing in there, but they really weren't using it the way I envisioned it. The third week I thought that it was probably time to close the center, but I thought I would give it a few more days. All of the sudden, two little boys were in there and they decided they were going to make it a sports office. They decided to sell tickets to Bucks games for two dollars. They made a drive-up window and they made little tickets. They actually had children standing in line waiting to purchase tickets. Then a girl joined them and decided to sell ballerina tickets. They had a great time playing in the sports office for another week and a half. There were frequently ten children playing and interacting there at a time. What they taught me was that they needed time to find out how the office worked for them in their world. What I envisioned for them was not at all what turned out to be important to them. It just surprised me as I was watching them. *[Messiness of data: Sometimes categories emerge that you weren't expecting. Be open to possibilities rather than trying to fit all data into neat categories. Patience and close observation allowed Lenore to discover the depth of her students' play.]*

JEN: Because I think you do almost get so—like the research part is, it just becomes your life. I started to forget, wait, why am I doing this in the first place? Forget that I'm working on my master's project. What do I want the kids to be doing? So I had to keep going back to that question.

SHARON: And what question am I trying to answer?

JEN: Right.

SHARON: What is it that I'm trying to find out, and is this going to help me? Because I don't know if this happened to you three, but it happened to me, that I'd have this focus, and then I would look at some data and I would think, wow, is that interesting. And then I'm going off in another direction. And I would have to keep bringing myself back. What question am I trying to answer? How is this piece of information going to help me answer this question; whether it supports what I want to have happen or not doesn't matter. How is it going to answer the question? In what way will it help me to answer the question? Then, yeah, and that structure is so important, then, just having that to refocus.

DEB: Right. And what you're saying has reminded me that there's not a danger in reporting discrepant cases. It's important to report them.

SHARON: Well, I think what you're bringing up is that, yeah, there are all sorts of variables. For instance, I can give you an example, and tell me if I'm on the same page with you here. When we looked at development of empathy in children, you know, based on these intergenerational experiences, all of our kids—except for one, let's say—come from homes where they talk about these experiences and whatever, whatever. Then we might have one student who comes from a home where there is severe neglect or severe abuse or whatever. So we might have all of this data to support that these intergenerational experiences have this positive impact on the development of empathy. But, good heavens, here we have this one kid who actually gets worse or whatever. So, right, we need to report that. But then perhaps this is why. We have to give that perhaps. Because, right, it doesn't make what we're seeing any less true. It just means that we're also seeing this and here are the gazillion other variables that we can't control. We don't have a control group setting here. Is that what you mean? *[Discrepant cases: Reporting of discrepant cases increases the validity of the study. We know children learn differently. Reporting of discrepant cases acknowledges these differences and reflects the objectivity of the researcher.]*

DEB: Yes. And I was thinking, in terms of, as a teacher, the fact that discrepant cases would exist doesn't surprise me at all. I would expect to find them. I would be surprised if everything pointed to the same kind of effectiveness for everybody.

SHARON: Right. And it adds to the whole, you know, children aren't cookie cutouts of each other. Every person is this unique little package with all these variables from their home environment, their experiences, their genetic makeup, all these things that not only can we not control, we don't even know what they all are, they're so vast. And looking at those I think actually adds to the validity.

DEB: Right.

JEN: And that's why action research to me makes so much more sense in education. Because there's no way you're ever going to duplicate an experiment anyway. What I did last year, I'm doing again this year. But I'm doing it differently because I had to change it a little bit. And, you know, they're different kids and I'm getting different results anyway. And you just can't—it would be inaccurate, I think, to say, well, if you do this, this will happen. You can't say that. Because even in your own classroom, you can't say, because I did this, this happened for everyone.

SHARON: I think the one piece that we do have to look at kind of goes back to the theoretical underpinnings of whatever it is that you did because that's the piece that does remain constant. There are certain truths about human development. I don't know if " truth" might be a little strong word. But there are theories out there, and as educators, what we need to do is be very, very aware of just what you brought up, that these kids are all different. They all have different backgrounds, and from this particular group of students at this particular point in time, based on what I've read, I know that this is the best way to do this particular project or paper or program or whatever. And next year, I have different kids and I know that, for instance, me, with the intergenerational programming, intergenerational programs that have been successful have this, this, this, and this in common. So, now I'm going to do these things, but as it makes sense for this particular group of kids that I have. And, yeah, I think that for us in education, for us to do research based on some kind of a clinical model is totally ludicrous, because we don't operate in the real world that way. We need to know, and I think that people reading our research need to understand, that this research is valid in this setting. For this group of students at this time, this is true. Take from it what you will and use it with your group of students, you know. And it's the art of teaching, of course.

CONCLUSION

Action research can be a powerful tool to improve teaching practice. The kind of reflection required is the same as that encouraged by the National Board for Professional Teaching Standards. As more teachers undertake action research projects, serious questions need to be raised: How can teachers ensure that their results are valid? Are teachers drawing conclusions supported by their data? The four teachers included here used various methods to ensure that they were drawing trustworthy conclusions in their projects. I have synthesized their strategies into four principles.

1. *The research question must have integrity.* The project must begin with a question that can be answered by using the action research process. One can ask, "Can the question be adequately answered by implementing the procedures and by collecting data?" A teacher wanted to know the effects of a parent education program on the reading achievement of second graders. She proposed providing four parent education sessions and then checking for improvement in reading scores. Her question posed problems with validity. Would four sessions be enough to affect parents' understanding and use of certain reading strategies? How would the teacher know how well the strategies were being used? How would the teacher know how much the parents' interventions were affecting reading achievement and how much that achievement was influenced by her own instruction? Clearly, the findings of this study would not have had integrity. By changing the question, she was able to investigate her own efforts in setting up and implementing the parent education program.

A good research question has ramifications throughout the study. It's important to revisit the question frequently to check on your focus. Are your procedures evolving out of the question? Is your data analysis answering the question? You can change the question if your study suggests that you should ask a different question.

2. *A review of literature undergirds the action research project.* The four teachers used their literature reviews to inform their projects. By looking at studies and theories related to their projects, they found practical suggestions for their projects' implementation. Other studies reassured them that their procedures would produce valid results. They found help in designing methodologies that would effectively accomplish the goals that they had set for their projects. They also learned what data collection methods were used by researchers with similar questions. Two of the teachers used theoretical frameworks from the literature to analyze their data. Besides being useful, the review of literature helps to ensure validity by grounding the action research in more academic research.

3. *Triangulation promotes validity.* The teachers collected a lot of data from various sources. They asked, Have enough data been collected? before they ended their studies. Triangulation is essential to the validity of any action research project. Teachers must use at least three sources of data from which to draw conclusions. Like all qualitative researchers, the four teachers kept a journal in which they wrote objective and reflective comments. They collected student work, videotaped and audiotaped class discussions and work, created checklists, conducted interviews, took surveys, and gave pre- and posttests. Because they found consistent patterns throughout their data, they were assured that they had uncovered something that really happened in their classrooms. When they found disconfirming evidence, they thought about what had caused the inconsistencies.

4. *Drawing valid conclusions requires careful, thoughtful processing.* The four teachers used sound reasoning to draw conclusions and carefully reported their results. They examined and reexamined the data, sometimes asking others to help them. They questioned, What am I really seeing? Do the conclusions follow logically from the data? Just as the procedures and data collection methods must flow from the question, the conclusions must spring from the data. They

avoided overgeneralizations. They reported their findings in ways that allowed their readers to understand the contexts in which they worked. They reported discrepant cases, reflecting their objectivity and enriching their analysis. They took caution not to claim causality by using phrases like "the data seem to indicate" or "the data suggest."

As action research becomes a significant tool to improve teacher practice, care must be taken to ensure that teachers, using this research model, are getting valid results and drawing valid conclusions. Quantitative research does not provide a useful paradigm for thinking about validity. Action researchers will find qualitative research a more fruitful model. However, action research requires its own theory of validity, for action researchers do undertake "action," unlike many qualitative researchers who observe and reflect in naturalistic settings. These four teachers not only investigated their research questions but also considered ways to make certain that they would have trustworthy results.

7

Value of Action Research

The value and validity of action research are topics that have been hotly contested. Criteria for validity have been debated by academics with differing viewpoints. The criteria for the value of action research, however, can best be determined by the ways in which it affects students and teachers. In this chapter, we turn to the teachers again to hear how action research has changed their lives and their classrooms. This book has been written about teachers and for teachers, so it is appropriate that we listen to the individual voices of the four action researchers once more.

TEACHER VOICES

Deb: "I Feel Like I Developed So Many Skills"

I could probably talk forever about what I learned during the project and what impact it had on me! Because the project demanded at least some content integration, I knew immediately that I would be better off if I had more knowledge of physics. I'm sure there were opportunities to connect concepts that I totally missed because I didn't know enough about the physics concepts. I also realized the importance of content knowledge because I chose to sequence topics differently than they are traditionally presented. Mathematics is very sequential. A teacher has to know what topics can be shuffled without adverse affects.

I became more aware of simple conversations I had with students about math. I listened to what they were saying or asking about a problem or process, because I was conscious of always collecting data. I became aware of how articulate they could be and how self-aware many of them were in terms of their own understanding of the concepts. I recognized that this careful, data-collection listening was actually also a means of informal, ongoing assessment.

As I mentioned earlier, I have continued to use what, for the project, were data-collection methods (student writing) to help foster and assess understanding.

I think I have incorporated the basic structure of action research (raise a question related to a learning goal, gather information and ideas, create and implement a plan based on those ideas, carefully observe and assess results, and make adjustments based on findings) into how I plan lessons. The notion of student understanding has also become an ever-present, primary goal for me. I am always thinking about what I can do or what I can have the students do to promote real understanding of the concepts. I think the process of action research changed my whole view of teaching and learning.

After completing an action research project, I felt ready to tackle the process of National Board certification, and while [I was] engaging in that process, the similarities to action research were very apparent. I believe that my success with the certification process was directly related to my experience with action research.

Several things I knew about myself were definitely confirmed throughout the action research process. I'm a perfectionist and I'm obsessed with learning. I loved doing the review of literature. I was finally doing research that was practical and would affect what I did in the classroom. I was struck by how long I had spent reinventing the wheel instead of looking for teaching ideas from others. It was hard for me to stop reading and start writing. In addition to an undergraduate major in mathematics, I also had a major in psychology, and my interest in learning theory was rekindled as a result of doing action research.

As a psychology major, I was required to conduct a scientific study, including control group, experimental group, and so on. I was always uncomfortable trying to apply that kind of research to the classroom. Who are we kidding? How much "control" does a teacher have over all the variables that affect student learning? Action research acknowledged the subjective nature of classroom research, and that just made so much more sense to me.

I feel like I developed so many skills while completing the project. I had to develop organizational systems in order to manage all the information. I certainly honed my writing skills and became a more efficient researcher.

Since I completed my master's-degree action research project, I pursued coursework toward a Ph.D. in education. The skills I learned doing action research have served me very well in this endeavor. I have carried over my interest in student understanding and communication into the work I will do (another action research project) for my dissertation.

Jen: "An Overwhelmingly Positive Experience"

It's difficult to explain the impact this project had on me. It was an overwhelmingly positive experience for me—and, I think, for my students and colleagues. I felt a real sense of empowerment through this process, because of the large amount of research required and because of the freedom allowed me in terms of the design of my project. I felt truly ready to design the project, because of all the reading and research I had done, and I loved the qualitative focus of the project. It was actually quite a relief to know that I *could not* claim cause and effect, because all educators know there is no way anyone could ever duplicate a study—there are too many variables outside our control. Knowing that I "just" had to present my research, explain my procedures, and present my findings in "thick, rich description" (although this was a lot of work) alleviated the pressure I felt to design the "perfect project" for others to imitate. This process has made me more confident and willing to try new things in my classroom, because I know that if I base my decisions in research and just try new methods/assignments, and so on, whatever happens, happens; I can adjust what didn't work and take what did work.

My students also seemed excited about being part of the study, and about developing skills they could use in every class. They did get a little sick of all the planning and goal setting I had them doing, but several of them did use the strategies for work in other classes. It made me realize that we need to more explicitly teach and require the use of metacognitive skills, and we need to develop these skills in our students at the appropriate times. For example, in terms of English classes, perhaps we need to really focus on the metacognitive skills of planning and goal setting with our ninth graders, and work on the metacognitive skills of drafting and revising in tenth and eleventh grade.

This process also allowed me to share my new knowledge and excitement with my colleagues, so that, perhaps eventually, these metacognitive skills will become as important as the traditional content area skills.

I cannot say enough about the process of completing a qualitative research project. I feel more confident and knowledgeable as a teacher and colleague in the education profession, and I feel a stronger sense of my responsibility, as an educator, to ensure that all my students learn the skills that will help them succeed in every class, not just my own.

Sharon: "I Think I'm More Directed and Focused in Thought"

Since the project, I very often look at new situations, curricula, initiatives, plans, ideas, clubs, programs, and so on in terms of:

- *Previous research:* what's already out there to support the decisions we're making and to affirm that the direction we're headed in makes sense for us.
- *Phases:* researching, planning, implementing, evaluating, drawing conclusions. I think I'm more directed and organized in thought, more efficient and effective working with new initiatives, with teachers and with children because I can more clearly see the situation at hand as a process with various steps involved. There is a sense of order to things now that helps me set priorities and feel less overwhelmed.
- *"Results expected":* I consider and question, in the planning and implementation phases, how we will know if we've achieved our goal. Working from a "results expected" mindset helps me, again, to prioritize and to think in a more logical, organized, and, consequently, more effective and efficient manner. This perspective also helps me to consider more clearly how my actions/decisions might personally impact those around me.

I've always believed that the purpose of education is to promote effective citizenship in our democracy and world. My conviction that effective citizenship is based on the development of a strong personal sense of self and a strong positive view of self as a member of the community has been affirmed. Our efforts as educators to promote academic success should be carried out with the end goal of promoting effective citizenship.

Lenore: "It Truly Changed and Strengthened the Way I Teach"

This project was the most powerful professional development method I have ever encountered. It truly changed and strengthened the way I teach. It gave me a deeper understanding of emergent literacy development in young children and a clearer vision of my role in their literacy development.

Although the research was immense, it was extremely beneficial. It gave me new insights into my teaching strategies. Based on the research, I was able to adjust my strategies and make them more effective. I learned to become a more careful observer and facilitator. My teacher-directed activities became more focused, yet more encompassing. I became more aware of the direction I wanted to lead students with regard to literacy development, but I also became more flexible in letting student interest guide my instruction. I began to view literacy as part of our classroom culture rather than merely a subject to be taught. It became an integral part of my classroom management, routines, and procedures. I also learned that it was vital for me to reassess my views from time to time in order to keep developmental appropriateness in the forefront on my decision making.

Overall, the project went very well. I was amazed at the literacy behaviors four-year-olds already had in place, when given the opportunity and literacy props. At times throughout the project, it was exhausting and overwhelming, but in the end it was a very empowering journey! Four years later, it is still one of the best things I have ever done professionally and continues to have a positive impact in my classroom.

CONCLUSION

Not all action research projects affect teachers to the degree that Deb's, Jen's, Sharon's, and Lenore's have changed their teaching and their lives.

Deb's action research project became the springboard to National Board certification and the pursuit of a doctorate in education. Most teachers are not inspired to direct their energies in those ways. However, many teachers find that action research changes them as teachers. They gain a sense of empowerment when they see how they can change their practice and thereby influence student learning. Teachers realize that there are many variables in the classroom that they can't control. Events ranging from children not getting enough sleep because of gunshots in the night to hot and humid classrooms in June have an impact on children's learning, yet teachers cannot change these circumstances. However, teachers can change their own practice.

Deb learned the importance of focusing on student understanding—how to promote and assess it. She realized the importance of listening to students talk about their learning. Her lesson planning now is modeled on the research process, beginning with asking a question about learning.

Jen became more confident in herself as a teacher and as a leader in her department. She recognized that students need to be taught thinking skills, especially metacognition, in an explicit way. She is now working with her English department to infuse these skills into the curriculum.

Sharon now looks at different kinds of problems as research problems. She has learned that the research process can be applied to various situations by focusing on the problem, prioritizing, planning, and implementing. By considering the expected results in the planning phase, Sharon has become a more efficient problem solver.

Lenore's teaching has been transformed by action research. She sees herself and her students differently. She understands the importance of letting students' interests guide their learning and her role as a facilitator of that process. Literacy has become part of the culture of her classroom.

These teachers are just a few of the many teachers who have undertaken the journey of action research. Through a continuous process of planning, action, and reflection, they made significant differences in the lives of the children they taught. The completion of each of their action research projects led to new questions and new ideas for future projects.

During their projects there were bumps and potholes as well as beautiful vistas. There were moments of panic and frustration along with feelings of satisfaction and confidence. However, for them, as well as for you, it is the totality of the journey, not just the destination, that is the ultimate reward.

References

American Federation of Teachers, and National Education Association. (2001–2002). *A candidate's guide to National Board certification.* Washington, D.C.

Anderson, G., Herr, K., and Nihlen, A. (1994). *Studying your own school: An educator's guide to qualitative practitioner research.* Thousand Oaks, Calif.: Corwin.

Best, J. W., and Kahn, J. V. (1998). *Research in education* (8th ed.). Boston: Allyn and Bacon.

Brooks, J. G., and Brooks, M. G. (1993). *In search of understanding: The case for constructivist classrooms.* Alexandria, Va.: Association for Supervision and Curriculum Development.

Caine, R. N., and Caine, G. (1991). *Making connections: Teaching and the human brain.* Menlo Park, Calif.: Addison-Wesley.

Calhoun, E. F. (1994). *How to use action research in the self-renewing school.* Alexandria, Va.: Association for Supervision and Curriculum Development.

Carr, W., and Kemmis, S. (1986). *Becoming critical: Education, knowledge, and action research.* Philadelphia: Falmer.

Cochran-Smith, M., and Lytle, S. (1993). *Inside/outside: Teacher research and knowledge.* New York: Teachers College Press.

Dewey, J. (1929). *The sources of a science of education.* New York: Liverright.

Eisenhart, M., and Howe, K. (1992). Validity in qualitative research. In M. LeCompte, W. Millroy, and J. Preissle (eds.), *The handbook of qualitative research in education* (pp. 643–680). San Diego, Calif.: Academic Press.

Fraenkel, J. R., and Wallen, N. E. (1990, reprinted 2003). *How to design and evaluate research in education.* New York: McGraw-Hill.

Gardner, H. (1983). *Frames of mind: A theory of multiple intelligences.* New York: Basic Books.

Glickman, C. D., Gordon, S. P., and Ross-Gordon, J. M. (1998). *Supervision of instruction: A developmental approach* (4th ed.). Boston: Allyn and Bacon.

Goetz, J. P., and LeCompte, M. D. (1984). *Ethnography and qualitative design in educational research.* New York: Academic Press.

Goldhaber, J., Lipson, M., Sortino, S., and Daniels, P. (1996–1997). Books in the sandbox? Markers in the blocks?: Expanding the child's world of literacy. *Childhood Education, 73,* 88–91.

Grady, M. P. (1998). *Qualitative and action research.* Bloomington, Ind.: Phi Delta Kappa Educational Foundation.

Guba, E. G. (1981). Criteria for assessing the trustworthiness of naturalistic inquiries. *Educational Communication and Technology, 29*(2), 75–91.

Guba, E. G., and Lincoln, Y. S. (1981). *Effective evaluation.* San Francisco: Jossey-Bass.

Hiebert, J., Gallimore, R., and Stigler, J. (2002). A knowledge base for the teaching profession: What it would look like and how can we get one? *Educational Researcher, 31,* 3–15.

Hodgkinson, H. (1982). Action research: A critque. In S. Kemmis (ed.), *The action research reader* (2nd ed., pp. 64–68). Geelong, Australia: Deakin University Press.

Huberman, M. (1996). Moving mainstream: Taking a closer look at teacher research. *Language Arts, 73,* 124–140.

Kemmis, S. (1982). Action research in retrospect and prospect. In S. Kemmis (ed.), *The action research reader* (2nd ed., pp. 11–31). Geelong, Australia: Deakin University Press.

Lincoln, Y. S., and Guba, E. G. (1985). *Naturalistic inquiry.* Beverly Hills, Calif.: Sage.

Maxwell, J. A. (1992). Understanding and validity in qualitative research. *Harvard Educational Review, 62*(3), 279–300.

Mills, G. E. (2000). *Action research: A guide for the teacher researcher.* Upper Saddle River, N.J.: Merrill.

Morrow, L. M., and Rand, M. K. (1991). Promoting literacy during play by designing early childhood classroom environments. *The Reading Teacher, 44,* 396–402.

Neuman, S. B., and Roskos, K. (1990). Play, print, and purpose: Enriching play environments for literacy development. *The Reading Teacher, 44,* 214–221.

Reason, P., and Rowan, J. (eds.) (1981). *Human inquiry: A sourcebook of new paradigm research.* New York: John Wiley.

Richardson, V. (ed.) (2001). *Handbook of research on teaching* (4th ed.). Washington, D.C.: American Educational Research Association.

Rosenblatt, L. (1978). *The reader, the text, the poem: The transactional theory of the literary work.* Carbondale, Ill.: Southern Illinois University Press.

Sanford, N. (1981). A model for action research. In P. Reason and J. Rowan (eds.), *Human inquiry: A sourcebook of new paradigm research* (pp. 173–181). New York: John Wiley.

Smith, M. L., and Glass, G. V. (1987). *Research and evaluation in education and the social sciences.* Englewood Cliffs, N.J.: Prentice-Hall.

Stringer, E. T. (1996). *Action research: A handbook for practitioners.* London: Sage.

Suter, W. N. (1998). *Primer of educational research.* Boston: Allyn and Bacon.

Vukelich, C. (1993). Play: A context for exploring the functions, features, and meaning of writing with peers. *Language Arts, 70,* 386–392.

Wang, M. C., and Palincsar, A. S. (1989). Teaching students to assume an active role in their learning. In M. C. Reynolds (ed.), *Knowledge base for the beginning teacher* (pp. 71–84). New York: Pergamon.

Wiggins, G., and McTighe, J. (1998). *Understanding by design.* Alexandria, Va.: Association of Supervision and Curriculum Development.

Zeichner, K., and Noffke, S. (2001). Practitioner research. In V. Richardson (ed.), *Handbook of research on teaching* (4th ed., pp. 298–330). Washington, D.C.: American Educational Research Association.

About the Author

Eileen M. Schwalbach, Ph.D., associate professor of education, directs the graduate program in education at Mount Mary College in Milwaukee, Wisconsin. Dr. Schwalbach received a master of arts in English and a doctorate in urban education from the University of Wisconsin, Milwaukee. Her interest in action research began when she was an English teacher for the Milwaukee Public Schools. Her dissertation was an action research project that explored her high school students' use of a metaphor strategy in oral and written language. This work earned her the Jarvis Bush Techniques in Teaching Composition award from the Robert C. Pooley Foundation. She has published in research journals and presented nationwide on the topic of action research. She works individually with graduate students, who are conducting action research in their classrooms, as well as with teams of teachers from schools that are working on whole school reform.

DATE DUE

APR 2 8 '05		
MAY 0 6 '05		